Mary Kay

Mary Kay

MARY KAY ASH

1817

HARPER & ROW, PUBLISHERS, New York
Cambridge, Philadelphia, San Francisco,
London, Mexico City, São Paulo, Sydney

Library of Congress Cataloging in Publication Data

Ash, Mary Kay.
  Mary Kay.

  1. Mary Kay Cosmetics. 2. Ash, Mary Kay. 3. Cosmetic industry—United States—Biography. I. Title.
HD9970.5.C674M372   381'.456685'0924 [B]   81–47219
ISBN 0-06-014878-0   AACR2

81 82 83 84 85 10 9 8 7 6 5 4 3 2

Dedicated to the thousands of women who
DARED
to step out of their "comfort zones" and
USE
their God-given talents and abilities,
realizing that God did not have time
to make a nobody—
just a
SOMEBODY!

Contents

Photographs follow pages 82 and 146

Acknowledgment

I would like to gratefully acknowledge Bob Shook for his invaluable assistance in preparing this manuscript. Without his powers of organization and sincere encouragement, the Mary Kay story would probably never have been written.

Preface

Once before I started to write a book, shortly after I had retired from a twenty-five-year career in direct sales. I hadn't
been retired a week when I knew why so many obituaries
read: "He retired last year." I found I had no reason to get out
of bed in the morning.

In the years that I had worked, I had encountered many
problems. I thought my experience could perhaps help other
women over these same hurdles. To organize my thoughts, I
began by writing down all the good things the companies I
had worked for had done. I hoped doing that would clear my
heart of the bitterness I felt just then, and it did. After writing
for two weeks, I didn't feel nearly so bad about the opportunities that had been denied me just because I was a woman. The
next two weeks I spent writing down all the problems I had
encountered during those years. It was a long list, and I began
to think about a "dream company" that would be based on the
golden rule and offer women unlimited opportunities. Well,
those notes from that book which I never did write were the
very beginning of Mary Kay Cosmetics. The company was
founded on Friday, September 13, 1963; and now, eighteen
years later, I'm writing my book again. With the help of God
and my wonderful family, friends, and associates, Mary Kay
Cosmetics has grown from a little storefront company with

nine saleswomen to an international family of more than 100,000 Beauty Consultants. And, most important, the solutions I came up with have given thousands and thousands of women the opportunity to become so much more than they ever thought they could be. As founder and chairman of Mary Kay, I've received quite a lot of publicity. Now when I have something to say, people seem to listen. It's not that I'm saying anything any different from what I've said all my life. Apparently, when a person achieves some success, what he or she has to say becomes more important.

I've never been one to pass up an opportunity. So as often as I can, you'll hear me talking about the many wonderful opportunities in this world for women. And, while some of my philosophy is old-fashioned—employing the golden rule and what we have come to call the "Go-Give" spirit—it's also a "Yes, you can!" philosophy which I think is very much in tune with today's woman. And most importantly, it works! I want to share with you my philosophies, my inner feelings, my disappointments, and my joys. You will probably notice that I won't give too many dates. Of course I remember dates—like my children's birthdays! I'm a woman, and what woman isn't sentimental about those things? But if you had just a few dates, with a little arithmetic you'd know my age. I'm not as old as some people seem to think (I've heard rumors that I'm 82!), but why should I tell my age? A woman who will tell her age will tell anything! The best thing I ever heard on that subject was this: If you really didn't know how old you are—how old would you say you were? I feel 24!

Mary Kay

⚞ 1 ⚟
You Can Do It!

When I was seven years old, my daddy came home from the sanatorium. His tuberculosis had been arrested but not completely cured in his three years there, and he remained an invalid for the rest of my years at home, in need of a great deal of tender, loving care.

My mother was the sole support of our family for all those years. She managed a restaurant in Houston, working fourteen hours a day, leaving home each morning at 5:00 before I awoke, and returning about 9:00 P.M.—for many of those early years, after I was asleep. It was not a job that paid as well as such jobs do today, and undoubtedly she was paid less because she was a woman. Somebody had to take care of my daddy, and my older brother and sister were grown and gone. So the responsibility became mine.

It never occurred to me that things should be any different. I would come home from second grade and clean the house, and of course do my homework. But I accepted this—and more than that, I enjoyed it. Nobody ever told me I wasn't supposed to, even though some things were hard for me at that age. One of them was cooking.

My mother was a marvelous cook. But she couldn't be home to make our family dinner, so that became my job. As you can imagine, at the age of seven I didn't know much about preparing a meal. If Daddy wanted chili or chicken or whatever for dinner, and I didn't know how to cook it, I would call my mother. During those days, I rarely had the opportunity to learn anything from her in person—she just couldn't be there to teach me. But how often I have said since then, "Thank God for the telephone!" That was my lifeline during those years, and my main contact with my mother. Whenever I called her, she found a way to make time for me, and to explain patiently what I had to do.

"Mother, hi! Daddy wants potato soup tonight."

"Potato soup? Okay, honey. First you get out the big pot, the one you used yesterday. Then you take two potatoes . . ."

She'd go through every single step, one at a time, trying to think of everything I would need to know. I hadn't been raised to be a complainer, but I'm sure she knew that this sometimes seemed overwhelming. Because when she was through with her instructions, she always added, "Honey, *you can do it.*"

Our family situation made it necessary for me to do some things that most children aren't expected to do. For instance, I had to go to downtown Houston on the streetcar on Saturdays to buy whatever clothing I might need. I went alone, since my best friend was not allowed to go downtown on the streetcar without an adult—after all, we were seven years old!

Mother would give me perhaps $1.50—remember, this was in a day when a little girl's dress was sixty cents and eggs were nineteen cents a dozen! And I would go pick out a dress or blouse. I loved doing this—it was the highlight of my week. The only problem I had was convincing the clerks that I really was allowed to make such decisions. Sometimes it was enough to show them the money, but often they would demand, "Where's your mother?" Then I would explain and give them the phone number where she worked and tell them, "You can call her, she'll tell you it's okay."

But I loved those Saturday trips, because after I shopped I got to go to Kress's and get a pimento-cheese sandwich on toast and a Coke, and then go to the movie. And that was what I lived for. I think the meal was twenty cents and the show was about ten cents, so for thirty cents I had a wow of an afternoon!

I do remember that when I first started going downtown, I was a little anxious about catching the right streetcar and finding my way around. Then I remembered my mother saying, "You can do it, honey." I must have heard those words thousands of times, and she always said them with total conviction. Now I realize that she must have sometimes felt a little nervous herself about the responsibilities I had to assume. But you would never have known it to hear her. As far as I was concerned, my mother *knew* I could do it. Her words became the theme of my childhood, and they have stayed with me all my life: "You can do it."

The confidence my mother instilled in me has been a tremendous help. Without it, Mary Kay Cosmetics might have fizzled before it began. I had developed a strategy and a philosophy for my dream company, and invested my life savings in it. Several salespeople had been recruited. We had boxes of bottles and jars and brand-new labels reading Beauty By Mary Kay. (This was later changed to Mary Kay Cosmetics, Inc.) Everything was ready to go. Using my years of experience in direct sales, I would work with the Beauty Consultants, while my husband (I had married again) would run the administrative end of the business. Then, one month to the day before we were scheduled to open, my husband and I were having breakfast, and he was reading the final percentage figures. I was listening very much like a woman does when her husband is talking about the budget—with half an ear, feeling that was "his problem." At that moment, he suffered a fatal heart attack.

I believe that work is often the best antidote for grief. And, despite my shock, I had to make a decision about Mary Kay Cosmetics. The company was my dream and my idea, but I had never planned to run it alone. I knew I didn't have the skills or experience for the administrative end. And yet, all the merchandise and bottles and labels were useless if the company folded now. I *had* to go on.

I turned to my attorney and accountant for their advice.

"Mary Kay," my attorney told me, shaking his head, "liquidate the business right now and recoup whatever cash you can. If you don't, you'll end up penniless."

My accountant, I hoped, would be a little more encouraging. He studied the situation while I watched him. "You can't possibly do it," he said. "This commission schedule will never work. It's just a matter of time before the company goes bankrupt—and you along with it."

The day of the funeral, my sons and my daughter came to Dallas from Houston. Perhaps it was the worst possible time to make a decision like this, but it could not be delayed for long. After the funeral, we sat in my living room and talked it over, and I told them what my attorney and accountant had said. They listened in silence.

Richard was just then selling life insurance for Prudential. At twenty, he was one of the youngest agents in Texas. He was being paid $480 a month, a figure I thought was ridiculous—he was just a kid! I couldn't offer him anything like that. But I needed him if Mary Kay Cosmetics was to become a reality. I took a deep breath and offered him $250 a month to come with me and help me guide the new company. He accepted without hesitation, and immediately moved to Dallas over the horrified protest of other family members and friends.

Ben, who was seven years older, was employed by a welding company, and was married and had two children. He was not in a position to pull up roots and join the company just then, but he said, "One day I'd like to join you and Richard."

Then, calmly and deliberately, he reached into his breast pocket and pulled out a savings passbook that showed a balance of $4,500. I knew that sum represented everything he had saved since his high school days.

"Mother," he said, "I think you could do anything in this world that you wanted to." He handed me the book. "Here's my savings. If this will help you in any way, I want you to have it."

Eight months later, when we needed someone to handle our expanding warehouse, Ben moved his family from Houston to join us. Giving up a salary of $750 a month, he started with the company at the same pay as Richard—$250 a month. (My daughter Marylyn later became the first director in Houston.) On Friday, September 13, 1963, one month after the funeral, Mary Kay Cosmetics opened on schedule. With myself, nine salespeople, and my twenty-year-old son as financial administrator, how did I know I could do it? I didn't. I had no crystal ball. But I *had* to do it. As for the predictions of my attorney and accountant, I figured they didn't have any crystal balls either—and besides, they didn't understand the business, and I did. I also knew that I would never have a second chance to put my dream into action. If Mary Kay Cosmetics folded, I was back in retirement. But I would be broke, so I would have to work for somebody else for the rest of my life. So no matter what anyone thought, I just couldn't give up my dream. My children had said, "You can do it." That was all I needed!

Richard and Ben knew what my advisers had said. And yet they had given their unqualified support. I never needed that kind of support more badly than I did on the day of the funeral; it reassured me and it filled me with new confidence.

"Mother," Richard had said gently, putting an arm around my shoulders, "Ben and I have talked about this. We've watched you all our lives make a success of everything you've done. If you could be successful working for somebody else, we know you can do even better working for yourself."

Of course, my children had grown up believing their

mother could do anything. I had been virtually their sole support from the time they were born until they were grown and
out on their own. They had watched me get up at five every
morning to catch up on my work and get them off to school,
and then go out to earn our living in sales. They knew I was
always there from the time they got home until I left again to
work until late at night. Over the years, the family had moved
to nicer houses and better neighborhoods, and they knew I
had managed that somehow. So, as children will, they grew
up thinking their mom could do anything.

It's just possible that at that time the boys had a little
more confidence in the Mary Kay dream than Mary Kay did. I
knew my way around in direct sales; and I knew the ideas I
had built into the company were terrific. But a company ad-
ministered by a twenty-year-old boy? Only yesterday Richard
had been a teen-ager who wanted nothing in the world more
than a motorcycle. Yes, he'd been a good student. But if he can
really help me operate a business successfully, I thought, it'll
be a miracle! I honestly couldn't see Richard replacing my husband in that role.

But I had mistrusted God. I should have known that
when God closes a door, He always opens a window. I might
not realize how much ability Richard had, but God did, and
He got Richard ready and placed him in the position. Five
years later, Richard was given the Man of the Year Award by
the American Marketing Association and, at that time, he was
the youngest man ever to receive the award. He was then
twenty-five. Later, when Mary Kay Cosmetics was listed on
the New York Stock Exchange, Richard became one of the
youngest persons ever to be president of a company listed on
the New York exchange. From the beginning, Richard was a
godsend. He ran the corporate business, from manufacturing
to marketing, leaving me free to spend my full time and energy directing and motivating the sales organization. We were
quite a team—and we still are. Today, I still depend on his

financial and administrative genius. He even balances my personal checkbook!

Despite the vital support of my sons, I don't think I could have ever gone ahead with Mary Kay when so many people advised me not to, if it hadn't been for the memory of my mother's belief in me. "You can do it," I'd say to myself, just as she had said it all those years.

But I'm not sure any of us can take the whole credit for the success of my dream. A friend of mine once said, "Mary Kay Cosmetics was a divine accident looking for a place to happen." In 1963, the women's movement had not yet begun—but here was a company that would give women all the opportunities I had never had. I don't think God wanted a world in which a woman would have to work fourteen hours a day to support her family, as my mother had done. I believe He used this company as a vehicle to give women a chance. And I feel very humble and very fortunate to have had a part in showing other women the way.

"You can do it!" is a daily theme at Mary Kay Cosmetics. So often a woman comes to us who desperately needs to hear that. Frequently she is a housewife who has been out of the job market for many years, or who has never worked outside the home. Now her children are older, and she feels empty and useless. She needs something to do that will make her feel valuable, but she has no skills to sell an employer. She may come under our wing very tentatively—she'll buy her beauty case, but she's really not sure . . .

When I see a woman like this, I want to do for her what nobody did for me, in the way of providing opportunities. I suppose I'm like a mother who wants to give her children the things she didn't have. The first thing such a person needs to hear is, "You can do it!" Sometimes nobody has ever told her that in her life. But we also make sure she learns the necessary skills. We encourage her to improve her appearance so she looks the part of a Beauty Consultant. And when she does that, she begins to improve in other ways, too. Her confidence builds. She becomes more efficient, and begins to set goals. Very often a Mary Kay career is a self-improvement program and a way of life—not just a way to earn money.

Of course, we don't take the credit for her success. When a shy Consultant turns out to be a top salesperson, *she's* the one who did it—we just provided her with some needed encouragement. And we don't take credit for her talent either. It was always there. She just wasn't aware of it. The sad truth is that 90 percent of all people—not just women—die with their music still unplayed. They never dare to try. Why? Because they lack confidence in themselves. It's sad. Women have so *much* potential many of them never tap. Grandma Moses is a great example. She didn't even begin painting until she was 78, yet in only four years, her works were exhibited at the Metropolitan Museum of Art in New York. That in itself was marvelous. But certainly she could have been painting for many, many years before that—she just never tried. Isn't that a shame? If she had only started painting earlier in her life, she could have left the world so much more of her beautiful work.

For me, the most meaningful thing about the growth of Mary Kay Cosmetics has been seeing so many women achieve. All of us here thrive on helping instill in other women the "You can do it!" spirit. So many women just don't know how *great* they really are. They come to us all *vogue* on the outside and *vague* on the inside. It's so rewarding to watch them develop and grow. A woman often comes in like a tight little rosebud; sometimes she appears at my door too inhibited to even tell me who she is. And the same woman coming back after six months of praise and encouragement is hardly recognizable. She has changed from a tight little bud into a beautiful rose, poised and confident.

At a recent meeting, I heard one Consultant say, "When I started working for Mary Kay, I was terrified to speak in front of six people. I didn't see how I was going to make it through my first Beauty Show." That same woman was on stage, smiling and radiant, that night, talking to eight thousand people! I think it's obvious that someone did a good job of telling her, "You can do it!" She probably didn't believe it the first time she heard it, and she didn't believe it the second time. But after a while, our women decide that *we* believe it, and pretty soon they believe it, too.

If you ever come to visit Mary Kay headquarters in Dallas, and you see someone wearing a diamond bumblebee pin, you can be sure she's a top performer in our company. The bumblebee has become the number-one symbol within our organization of women who have "flown to the top"! Some years ago, Mel, my late husband, gave me a diamond bumblebee pin, and everyone just loved it. Since it was so popular, I decided to present a pin like that every year to each woman who is crowned Queen of various categories at our annual Seminar.

It's a beautiful pin, but that isn't the whole story. We think the bumblebee is a marvelous symbol of woman. Because, as aerodynamic engineers found a long time ago, the bumblebee cannot fly! Its wings are too weak and its body is too heavy to fly, but fortunately, the bumblebee doesn't know that, and it goes right on flying. The bee has become a symbol of women who didn't know they could fly but they *DID*! I think the women who own these diamond bumblebees think of them in their own personal ways. For most of us, it's true that we refused to believe we couldn't do it. Maybe somebody said, "It's really impossible to get this thing off the ground." But somebody else told us, "You can do it!" So we did.

2

A Competitive Spirit

All through my childhood, my mother constantly told me, "Anything anyone else can do, you can do better!" After hearing that enough times, I became convinced that I *could* do better. One of the things she believed I could do was make straight A's—B's just weren't acceptable. After a while, I didn't want to disappoint my mother or myself. Before long, it wasn't just a matter of making the best grades in my class. I wanted to sell the most tickets for the May Fete, or the most boxes of Girl Scout cookies. Whatever I did, I wanted to excel! Of course I didn't always win. But my mother taught me how to lose. She encouraged me to look to the future: to do better the next time—to try harder. I think it's important for young people to learn that "you can't win 'em all." Being the best all the time just isn't possible. Today, when I see the strong emphasis placed on winning in some Little League teams, I just pray that someone is also teaching those youngsters how to accept defeat. Because anyone who competes has to face defeat sooner or later, and learn how to go on from there.

One of my favorite expressions is, "We fail forward to success." It's true—we learn from our failures. And how many times have we all heard it said that the person who never fails, never attempts anything? I've found that successful people aren't afraid to risk failure—and they do fail. I've told my

Consultants and Sales Directors countless times, "If we ever decide to compare knees, you're going to find that I have more scars than any in the room. Because I have fallen down and gotten up so many times in my life."

I was taught to put my best effort into anything I did, and I can honestly say I've always done that. Still, there were many times when I failed—many times when I was disappointed. We didn't set the world on fire from the first day; disappointments, setbacks, and work have created the company as it is today. I envisioned a company in which any woman could become just as successful as she wanted to be. The doors would be open wide to opportunity—for women who were willing to pay the price and had the courage to dream.

I believe you can have anything in this world you want—if you want it badly enough and you're willing to pay the price. All through my childhood, I heard that message: everything had a price. In order to get something, I had to give up something else. When I was young, that usually meant giving up an extra hour or two of sleep so I could study. When I began my sales career, I gave up more sleep, so I could do my housework and care for my children. And I gave up my social life, because there weren't enough hours in the day to work, keep house, look after the children, and have any time left over for anything else. But I wanted to support my family well, to buy a nicer house and move to a nicer neighborhood, and I knew that everything had a price.

The competitive spirit my mother had instilled in me kept me going through some very difficult days. I competed with myself. On Saturday, I wanted my earnings for the week to be a little more than the week before. When I was successful, it wasn't because I was any more talented than the next salesperson; I was just willing to make more sacrifices. I was willing to work hard, and pay the price for success.

Competing and striving to excel can be a lot of fun. As a child, I enjoyed the satisfaction of bringing home the A's my mother expected of me. And when I entered junior high school, I sampled more of the fun of competition. I discovered three talents: typing, extemporaneous speaking, and debating. Typing was my first challenge.

My typing teacher, Mrs. Davis, took me under her wing. I was determined to be the best typist in the class, and more than anything I wanted a typewriter of my own. But I knew it was way beyond our means, and it never occurred to me to ask for one.

Then one day my mother presented me with a Woodstock typewriter! To this day, I don't know how long it took her to pay for that typewriter, or how she managed to get together the money for a down payment. But it was like her to find a way; she would go to extraordinary lengths to encourage me to excel in whatever I did. She realized that having my own typewriter would help me to develop my skills. Needless to say, that old Woodstock typewriter was one of my most prized possessions. And knowing that my mother must have sacrificed to pay for it made me even more determined to become an expert typist. I had a great feeling of satisfaction when at last I was able to bring home a trophy for being the best typist in my class!

My other great ambition at that age was to be a good extemporaneous speaker, and again, a teacher encouraged me and coached me. Before I was out of junior high, I had competed in a statewide contest, and come in second in the whole state of Texas! In high school, I became interested in the debating team and became a member, and I won some honors there, too. I've never lost my love for extemporaneous speaking. Today, when I talk to thousands of women at Mary Kay meetings, I still get the same thrill I did back then. In fact, it's a bigger thrill!

The encouragement of my mother and my teachers was certainly very important. But as I look back on my childhood, I suspect the biggest influence on my competitive spirit was my childhood friend, Dorothy Zapp. Dorothy was not especially competitive herself, but being her friend gave me a vision of a whole other world that could be mine someday if I was willing to work for it. Of course, as a child I didn't really see it that way. I just enjoyed our friendship and all the privileges that came with it, and we are still friends today after all the intervening years.

Dorothy's circumstances were quite different from mine. Although she lived just around the corner, her house was by far the nicest one in the neighborhood, and her family was a world apart from mine. Dorothy wore little starched pinafores to school every day (remember, that was a long time before the days of wash and wear). Every morning her mother curled her long golden hair, and she always looked as though she had just stepped from the cover of a magazine. Then, little Mary Kathlyn would appear on the front porch to walk to school with picture-perfect Dorothy!

I still blame those mornings at Dorothy's house for the fact that I've been somewhat on the plump side ever since. Dorothy was a tiny, fragile child who never wanted to eat her breakfast. Her mother would coax her to eat her toast with strawberry jam and drink her tall glass of milk with ice. But when her mother wasn't looking, Dorothy would pass them over to me. Who was I to see that good food go to waste? And after all, Dorothy's breakfast was sumptuous fare compared to the bowl of cereal I had fixed for my breakfast.

Dorothy and I were only six weeks apart in age, and we were the best of friends. Since I was an *A* student, Mrs. Zapp considered me a good role model for Dorothy, and always welcomed me. As for me, it was a wonderful treat to be friends with Dorothy. It meant I was entitled to eat her delicious breakfast every morning, and to go on family vacations and trips to her grandmother's farm. And it meant I joined the family for Christmas festivities.

One of my fondest childhood memories is the beautiful Christmas tree the Zapps put up each year. It reached to the very high ceiling of their home, and it was magnificent. In those days, nobody used artificial ornaments. Instead, the Zapps' Christmas tree was strung with popcorn and cranberries and apples and oranges. To me, it was just the most beautiful Christmas tree in the world!

Although I didn't realize it at the time, my friendship with Dorothy made me more competitive. I was aware that I was supposed to be her role model, so, of course, I had to keep up the straight *A*'s. And when Dorothy made an *A*, I had to make an *A+*. This competition extended into other areas as well. If Dorothy sold twelve May Fete tickets, I had to sell twenty. Her friendship offered me so much that all I could do was try to excel at whatever I did. Even so, Dorothy and I willingly shared everything, and I don't think either one of us ever felt envy for the other. It was a wonderful friendship— and is to this day.

About the time we graduated from Dow Junior High, Dorothy's father got a promotion and the family moved to a larger house on the "right" side of town. I was so impressed that I still remember the address—4024 Woodleigh. After the move, we naturally didn't see as much of each other.

Another close friend was Tillie Bass, who lived across the street from me. Like Dorothy, Tillie came from a family that was much more affluent than mine. Her father was a chief of detectives in Houston, and I considered him a very important person. Tillie and her mother realized that I had to cook and keep house for my father, and they took me under their wing and taught me lots of things I needed to know. Tillie was eight years older than I was, so I had to strive to keep up with her. Back then, that eight-year difference in our ages made me feel that I had to do well to remain Tillie's friend—that I had to compete. Thank heaven, she didn't see it that way. To this day, we have remained good friends, and still get together often.

By the time I reached high school, my competitiveness was deep-rooted, and I continued exerting myself to make straight *A*'s. I would have liked to have been valedictorian, but I decided to finish high school in three years rather than four, and graduating from summer school ruined my chances. When we graduated, Dorothy went on to matriculate at Rice Institute, and I must admit to watching her with envy. College was something my family just could not afford, and in those days scholarships were rare.

What could I do to compete with the kids who went to college? It had to be something great. So I got married! I was only seventeen, and he was a big local radio star. (Television had not been invented.) He was part of a group called the Hawaiian Strummers, and I thought he was a tremendous catch—sort of Houston's Elvis Presley of that time. Maybe I couldn't go to college, but this was a real feather in my cap!

This was probably the first time the competitive spirit created a real problem for me, and led me to do something I would later regret. My young marriage was already unhappy when my young husband went off to serve in World War II. During the war years, I had to support and raise our three children alone. And when my husband returned, he announced he wanted a divorce. It was the lowest point of my life. I know many women will understand when I say I felt like a complete failure as a woman.

But with three children, I didn't have time to sit around feeling sorry for myself—I had to support my family. I wanted a job with flexible hours, so I could spend time with my children when they needed me. Direct sales was a natural solution, so I became a dealer for Stanley Home Products.

I enjoyed selling, but nothing excited me quite as much as company contests. It was just that competitive spirit of mine. I particularly remember one contest that really fired me up. The Stanley Home Products company announced that whoever recruited the most new people in a single week would be crowned Miss Dallas. Well, I figured that was the only way I would ever be Miss Dallas, so I was determined to win.

In those days, I was holding three Stanley parties* a day, and I had to generate enough sales to pay my bills. But I knew I couldn't hold all those parties and still win that recruiting contest, so I arranged for other Stanley dealers to take my place at the parties I had scheduled, and I concentrated on recruiting new people.

I figured I had one terrific source of possible recruits—my datebook. Since I had been holding so many parties, it was just crammed with the names of my hostesses. So I sat down and started calling. I telephoned every single hostess listed in my datebook, even those who had said no when I talked to them before, because I knew a woman's circumstances can change. So I called everyone.

I would say, "Hi, listen, Betty Ann, my company is planning to put on some more people in your area, and I got to thinking, 'Who do I know who would be just great doing what I do?' Well, naturally, I thought of you. Have you ever thought about going to work?"

"Well, Mary Kay, I just don't know . . ."

"Look, could I come by to see you this afternoon? I'm going to be out your way and I'd like to talk to you for a few minutes and bring you some literature to read. Would about two be convenient?"

All week I called former hostesses mornings, made appointments, and went to see them in the afternoons—I did nothing else. I wanted to win that contest! And I did, with seventeen recruits in one week! I still have that Miss Dallas ribbon. It doesn't look like much, but I was willing to give up a lot of sales commissions for a week to win it. As it turned out, I earned almost as much money as usual, because so many of the women I called said, "I'm glad you called, because I need . . ." or "My sister-in-law wants to have a party." So,

*A group sales presentation was referred to as a "party." As many as twenty-five people were invited to the home of a hostess, where the salesperson would demonstrate and sell Stanley Products.

there were actually lots of fringe benefits. But the fact is, I was perfectly willing to give up my income for a week to earn a ribbon that said Miss Dallas. Recognition was as vital to me as money.

When I set out to form my dream company, I remembered that incident. And I was convinced that I wasn't the only competitive woman around. I believed that other women would work hard for recognition, the way I did, even when sometimes they wouldn't work that hard for money. But I avoided designing contests in which each person had to compete with everyone else, and there could only be one or two or three winners. I am convinced that competition is most productive when you are competing with yourself.

In one company, we were awarded little loving cups for meeting a $1,000 monthly wholesale quota. I put them on the mantel until I ran out of space there, and then soon there were so many I would just put them in a box under my bed. I simply didn't know what to *do* with all of them. The only fun I ever had with them was when people would ask me, "What are all those loving cups for?" I'd answer, "For loving, of course, what else?"

Instead of loving cups, I thought, why not something pretty and useful? Why not golden goblets? And so in our company the Golden Goblet Club was formed.

The idea I began to form was very simple. The company would offer beautiful, gold-plated goblets, which were awarded for a $1,000 wholesale cash-in—in one month! When someone completed a set of twelve, she would then win a matching tray. After twenty, she would win a pitcher, so she would have a beautiful set for her dining room.

I went to Richard and enthusiastically told him all about it. "And all she has to do to win one," I said, "is sell $1,000 worth of wholesale merchandise in a month."

Richard looked at me with disbelief.

"We're dealing with *reality*," he said. "Our top people sell maybe $150 a week. And you're talking about selling $1,000 a month? Do you think they're going to do that for that stupid cup?"

You have to realize that this was back in the days when we were still publishing the names of people who sold $100 or more in a single week—all five people, that is. But I remembered the Miss Dallas contest. Recognition is the key, I thought.

"Yes, Richard," I said firmly, "they will work for it. This is going to be a very exclusive club. Only a few people will have a golden goblet. And they'll do it because they want the recognition the golden goblet represents."

"I think you've lost your mind," he said. And looking at it from a man's standpoint, you might also wonder who in the world would knock herself out to win a goblet—even if it was gold-plated!

But a lot of women did! They competed with themselves to win those goblets. After a year or two, we had to stop inscribing them, because there were just too many going out. Finally, some of our Consultants had accumulated 50 or more. We began getting inquiries as to whether the company would consider buying them back, because the Consultants just didn't have any use for scores of golden goblets!

Because of this, we finally discontinued the Golden Goblet Awards, but they had been a grand beginning. We initiated a new system called the Ladder of Success, which we still use today. It's based on the same principle: letting a woman compete with herself. Consultants and Sales Directors wear their Ladders of Success proudly. Everyone knows that a person with all diamonds on her ladder is a star performer. It's like wearing a straight-*A* report card on your lapel. At Mary Kay Cosmetics, we've never had contests in which there was a first, second, and third prize—and everyone else lost. I'd been through too many of those in my days with other direct sales organizations, and I'd seen people step on each other to win a contest. That kind of competitiveness is so destructive to morale within an organization that we've been very careful to avoid it altogether.

We have found that a woman loves to compete for recognition—when she is competing with herself. A long time ago, I realized that the wrong kind of competitiveness can create a destructive atmosphere in a company. I was once employed as a national training director for a direct sales company, and it was my job to travel to different cities and train the sales force. I used to say that what I needed most in that job was an asbestos suit, because when I went into a city there were so many fires to put out before I could get down to training. You can't *teach* people who are at each other's throats. The problems had to be solved first.

I think the competition we have at Mary Kay Cosmetics is very healthy. My own spirit of competitiveness has helped me accomplish many things in life. But I do believe in encouraging a person to compete with herself—here at Mary Kay Cosmetics, we've made that philosophy a company policy.

You know, Andrew Carnegie, the great industrialist, once said, "The first man gets the oyster, the second man gets the shell." That kind of competitiveness, where there's only *one* winner, may motivate some men, but I think it often has an adverse effect on others—and particularly on women. At Mary Kay Cosmetics, everyone has an opportunity to get the oyster, the shell, *and the pearl.* But we go a step further: instead of pearls, we award sapphires, rubies, and diamonds!

Today, Mary Kay Cosmetics is more than a post-retirement idea, wishful thinking, or a faraway dream. It's become a reality, and for me—a dream come true. The beautiful part is that it has made dreams come true for thousands of other women, too. That's success!

3

My Dream Company

I can honestly say that when I retired in 1963, the thought of starting my own company had never entered my mind. Yes, I had opinions about the organizations I'd worked for; there had been many things I thought should have been done another way, but I'm sure everyone feels this way at one time or another. However, I still never imagined I would start a company of my own.

After I retired, I decided to write my memoirs—actually, a book that would help other women overcome some of the obstacles I had encountered. First, I wrote down all of the good things the companies I had been with had done and then the changes I would make to create a company that was based on the golden rule. I began to dream of a company that would give women the opportunity to do anything in the world they were smart enough to do.

"Wouldn't it be *marvelous*," I kept thinking, "if someone would actually start such a company? I'd love to work for a company like this." And then I realized that I didn't have to just sit and wish—I could start that dream company because I had already discovered the ideal product. The skin care products that I loved and had been using faithfully for years would be *perfect* for my dream company.

I had discovered these products in the early '50s, at a

Stanley Home Products party. This particular party was attended by about twenty women, whose ages ranged from nineteen to seventy. As I demonstrated the Stanley Products, I kept looking at the women who were gathered there and wondering how it was possible for twenty women of such varied ages to *all* have peaches-and-cream complexions. Maybe it was the lighting in the room, I thought (this was the year that "pink light globes" had been introduced, with the promise that everyone would look as though they were in "candlelight").

After the Stanley party, we were gathered in the kitchen for coffee when I noticed the hostess handing out to the other women little white jars with black tops and penciled labels. As she did, she made notations in a composition book, and gave instructions: "Now, let's see, you've used number three for two weeks, so use number four for seventeen days."

This must be the secret of the beautiful complexions I saw there! Since the hostess had not offered me any of these creams, I asked, "What are you doing?" She explained that these people were her "guinea pigs" and that she felt she could take credit for everyone's skin in that room—except mine!

It took me a day or two to convince myself to even try the product. Finally I did give myself a facial. When my ten-year-old son, Richard, came home from school and gave me an "I'm home" kiss on the cheek, he said, "Gee, mom, you feel smooth!"

I asked her if *I* could become one of her "guinea pigs." She examined my skin carefully and discovered that I had a real whitehead problem and she added (in front of twenty women), "You have aging skin!" That wasn't too flattering— but I knew it was true. That night she gave me a shoe box and in it were the products that were the predecessors of today's "Basic Set" products. The Skin Freshener was in an old prescription-looking bottle and the other products were packaged in old reused jars. In the box was a direction sheet with terrible grammar and many misspelled words.

When I saw how the product was packaged, I must have looked a little dubious, because the women around me began telling me about improvements in their complexions in just a few short months. It was true that these women looked great now. In the back of my mind, I thought, "This just can't be all that good. She's really got these women brainwashed."

"Oh, come on," I said to myself. "It's just not possible to get results from *one* facial." But my face did feel wonderful.

It wasn't very long before I was a loyal fan of the skin care products, and I learned their origin. The woman I bought them from had received the formulation from her father, who was a hide tanner. He had noticed one day that his hands looked younger than his face. He was sure that the only reason for that was the tanning solutions he worked with every day. If they could turn big-pored, stiff hides into beautiful, small-pored, soft leather like a glove, perhaps they could do the same thing for your skin! So he began to experiment, using, in a modified form, some of the solutions on his face that he put on the hides. As a result, when he died at seventy-three, he had the skin of a much younger man.

He had proved his point, but no woman would ever do what he had done, for the process was time-consuming, smelly, and obnoxious. Everyone ridiculed his idea except his daughter. She supported his concepts, and later she moved to Dallas to become a cosmetologist. Starting with his formulation, she developed creams and lotions gentle enough for women. For ten years, she tried to sell them from her small in-home beauty shop. She died in 1961 without ever having achieved success.

I knew these skin care products would be perfect. My family and friends had been using them for many years, too, and I had seen the results. My own mother had started using them the same year I did.

She had been ill that year, and when I went to Houston for Thanksgiving, she felt so bad about her appearance that she wouldn't come out of her room. I left her a portion of my products, and said, "I don't know if it will help, but it's just done such great things for me. You can try."

She did try. She started to use it daily, just as I had instructed her to do, Night Cream, Cleansing Cream, the masque, the Skin Freshener, and the Day Radiance for daytime protection. When I went home for Christmas, my mother had become a firm believer, too. And, when she died at age eighty-seven, her skin was beautiful.

The skin care products had done wonderful things for mother and for me. In fact, everyone I knew who had used them had beautiful results. I decided to try to buy the formulations.

By this time, the woman who owned the formulations had died, and her daughter had taken over, but she, too, had never been able to market the product with the exception of selling to a few neighbors and friends. I made her an offer for the formulations, and she was very happy to sell them to me. I had a terrific product and what I thought was a great marketing concept. My dream company was about to become a reality!

When a man starts a business, he usually establishes monetary goals, such as, "We're going to do a hundred thousand dollars the first year." I'm often asked what my financial objectives were when we first started Mary Kay Cosmetics. Well, I didn't have any. My objective was to give women the opportunity to do anything they were smart enough to do. To me, P. and L. meant much more than profit and loss—it meant people and love!

Until my husband's fatal heart attack, he was to handle the administrative end of the business, and I was to be in charge of marketing. He often explained to me how we had to buy our goods at one price and sell them for X amount more to the customer. "That's how a business keeps from going broke, Mary Kay," he'd say. It just went in one ear and out the other.

I just wasn't interested in the dollars-and-cents part of the business. My interest was in offering women opportunities that in 1963 didn't exist anywhere else. The vast majority of companies then simply didn't have room for women in the executive suite. Sure, if a woman was really exceptional, she could become an assistant to a senior officer. But that was about as far as she could go. In my twenty-five years in the business world, I had seen countless capable individuals held back only because they were female.

I had been frustrated myself by the lack of opportunity for women. One company I worked for paid me $25,000 a year to be national training director. But the truth was, I was acting as national sales manager for much less than the job was worth. Then, too, there were times when I would be asked to take a man out on the road to train him, and after six months of learning the business from me, he was brought back to Dallas and made my superior at twice my salary! It really irked me when I was told that these men earned more because they had families to support. *I* had a family to support, too! It seemed to me that a woman's brains were worth only fifty cents on the dollar in a male-run corporation. And a woman's ideas were often not respected. It really upset me to present a good marketing plan and be dismissed with, "Mary Kay, you're thinking like a woman."

Having worked for several direct sales organizations, I knew what I wanted to do differently in my dream company. The first thing was to eliminate assigned territories. I remembered the time when I was earning $1,000 a month in commissions from my sales unit in Houston, and my husband took a new job in St. Louis. Since I couldn't take my Houston unit with me, I lost all the commission on the people I had recruited and trained and motivated for eight years. I thought this was totally unfair. Someone else inherited those Houston salespeople, and the commission on their sales—even though I had built the territory.

In Mary Kay Cosmetics, we don't have territories. A Beauty Consultant can be visiting Hawaii or California on vacation, or visiting her sister in Omaha, and recruit someone. If she does, even though she lives in Cleveland, she will always draw a commission from the company on the wholesale purchases of her recruit. The Omaha Director will take the visiting Consultant's new recruit under her wing and train her; she'll attend the Omaha sales meetings, and participate in the local sales contests. But even though that Omaha Director does all these things, the Cleveland Consultant who originally recruited the lady will get the commissions. We call this our "adoptee" program.

This Omaha recruit may go on to recruit people of her own, too. A good recruit, no matter where she lives, becomes the nucleus for additional people under the Consultant. As long as they're both active with the company, a Consultant will receive commissions from the company on her recruit's sales activity.

Just ask any financial adviser, and he'll tell you this system can't possibly work, but it does work! Today, Mary Kay Cosmetics has more than three thousand Sales Directors, and most Sales Directors in the country operate in more than one state—many in a dozen or more. Each Sales Director reaps the benefits from her recruits in other cities and helps other recruits in return.

From a typical man's standpoint, it just isn't feasible. "Why should anybody work to develop an adoptee—and never get a cent of commission on her? Why should *I* work to bring *your* person up the ladder of success, so *you* can get all the commissions? You're crazy!" he would say. But our Sales Directors don't think that way. Some of them have seventy-five to one hundred adoptees, and it does represent a drain on the energy of the Director. But our Sales Directors think, "I'm helping her, but someone else is helping *my* recruits in another city." And the system works. As far as I know, no other company has a system quite like this. I do think a company has to have an Adoptee System right from the very beginning.

However, when we started, one person after another told me it wouldn't work, but I said, "Yes, it will. It *will* work, because it's based on the golden rule." And it does.

Our entire philosophy at Mary Kay is based on the golden rule—we sometimes call it the Go-Give principle. We focus on *giving* instead of *getting,* not just in our Adoptee System, but in every aspect of the company. We use the Go-Give principle, for instance, in training our Beauty Consultants. We constantly stress that a Consultant should never have dollar signs in her eyes, thinking, "How much can I sell these people today?" Instead, think in terms of "What can I do so these women will leave here today feeling better about themselves? How can I help give them a better self-image?" We know that if a woman feels pretty on the outside, she becomes prettier on the inside, too—and goes home a better wife, a better mother, and a better member of the community.

When I planned Mary Kay Cosmetics, I wanted to give women the opportunity to buy their cosmetics in the best possible way, with the opportunity of trying them before they bought them. It wasn't long before I realized that most women don't understand *how* to take care of their skin. They buy a jar of this in the department store, and a jar of that in the drugstore, and something else some other place, completely uncoordinated. They really have no idea why they are using the products or what they do for the skin. And usually the products are not working together. I saw a real need for someone to teach skin care.

This was one reason I created the small Beauty Show, with no more than five or six women attending. At the time, other direct sales companies had "parties," asking the hostess to provide twelve to twenty-five people for the "sales demonstration." This presented all kinds of problems. Many hostesses felt their living rooms wouldn't hold that many people. Others would say, "I have to serve refreshments, and I don't even have that many cups!" But most of all, these large demonstrations were impersonal. I wanted our Consultants to work with small groups, so that each woman could be given personal attention. With five or six people at a Beauty Show, the Consultant could answer every question, and teach each woman what she wanted to know: for example, how to make her thin lips look fuller or how to make her round face appear more oval by contouring. In other words, personalizing the beauty process became our specialty. I wanted every woman to leave the Beauty Show knowing the best treatment for her individual skin, and the best way to make herself as pretty as she could be.

Since we wanted to *teach* skin care, retailing Mary Kay products in department stores was not the answer. Most women do not want to remove their makeup in a public place, nor is there time for a lengthy consultation, even if there's a makeup artist available. Then, too, the makeup artist is a professional. He or she can make you look like Elizabeth Taylor or Dracula, whichever he chooses, but once the customer takes that $100 worth of makeup home, she can't repeat what the makeup artist did. So I felt that the best way for a woman to buy cosmetics would be in a home environment, in natural light, with her own mirror and plenty of time to learn what to do. When a woman applies the makeup herself with a trained Consultant instructing her, she learns how to do it correctly. She can then repeat what she did that day. And she can do it over and over again, tomorrow and forever.

When a woman has this opportunity, she buys only what's best for her skin. Before I started using this skin care program, I think I was like most women—I had a lot of cosmetics in my dressing room that I never used. And I would never have bought them if I had had a chance to *try* them first! It's true that in most department stores there are all sorts of sample cosmetics out with mirrors. But really, it's very embarrassing to take off your makeup with people passing by, or even gathering around to stare! Most of us just won't do it. In addition, the lighting generally used in department stores is not ideal for true color selection.

At our Beauty Shows, we use a very low-key *educational* approach. We don't sell—we teach! I believe most women resent being "sold" in an aggressive manner. Our policy is to instruct. We present the products in an enthusiastic and knowledgeable manner, and teach women how to use them. And we offer an unconditional money-back guarantee. This is not only good for our customers, but our Consultants love it. We attract many, many women who couldn't pressure sell if they wanted to! And they don't want to. But they do like to *present*. They enjoy being skin care teachers.

In thinking about my dream company, I considered the problems other direct sales companies had. One big one was the problem of delivering two or three weeks after purchase. I think most women are impetuous. When I want something, I want it right now. I don't want to wait three weeks. In three weeks, I may not remember why I wanted it. In addition, when a company has a line of two hundred or three hundred products, there's no way the salesperson can have that inventory with her for immediate delivery. So we decided to limit the Mary Kay product line to a minimum of essential skin care and glamour items. Our beginning line consisted of about ten products. Even today, our line is streamlined—about forty products. We encourage each Consultant to keep a good inventory on hand for delivery at the Beauty Show. This way she can take an order, deliver, and collect the money the day of the Show. We don't require our Consultants to buy inventory, but those who do find that women will buy more readily when they can take it home with them.

In my dream company, I wanted to give women the maximum opportunity to earn. I wanted to pay the best commission possible. I thought and thought about how to do that, and finally came up with a policy that Mary Kay Cosmetics would deal with our salespeople on a cash basis. Bad debts are a major reason for failure in other direct sales companies. Many good sales representatives are lost not because they are dishonest, but because they are guilty of mismanagement.

At Mary Kay, our Consultants and Directors pay in advance for their merchandise with a cashier's check or money order—no personal checks. It's impossible for a Consultant to run up a debt with the company. Therefore, we have few accounts receivable. We don't have the expense of collecting bad debts, and we pass the savings on in the form of higher commissions. This way, everyone benefits. Most financial people just marvel at it—it's unheard of for a company of our size.

When I began Mary Kay, my accountant looked at my proposed commission structure and said, "There's no way, Mary Kay. You can't pay this many cents out of a dollar and still operate. It just won't work." But Richard worked it out and said it *would!*

My accountant was not the only disbeliever when I began talking about my dream. Many well-intentioned people, including my attorney, assured me it would fail. After all, who ever *heard* of a company based on the golden rule? My attorney went so far as to send to Washington for a pamphlet that showed how many cosmetics companies went broke every year. "Listen," people said, "you're *dreaming.*"

Yes, I was dreaming. That's how it all started. But when I look at what has happened in this company over the years, I am convinced it was not my dream alone. I believe that long before I sat down to write my memoirs and came up with a dream, God, in His infinite wisdom, had a plan to use my dream company—as a vehicle to help women all over the world. And instead of a door marked For Men Only, our company opened its doors wide with welcome—*especially* for women.

~ 4 ~
Mary Kay Cosmetics—
The Early Years

It's become traditional for the whole family to gather at my house on Thanksgiving Day. This past year there were going to be fifty-three of us, and I knew it would take the two biggest turkeys I could find to have enough for everyone. Unfortunately, my oven only holds one huge turkey. I *could* cook one turkey the day before, I thought, but if turkey isn't served on the day it's cooked, it seems to lose something. And, while I could cook one in the microwave oven, I really prefer slow cooking for a turkey.

Then I remembered something and went out to my garage. There, still sitting on a shelf, was my old turkey roaster. I dusted it off and tested it, and sure enough, it still worked. "Good old faithful," I thought, "you never did let me down." I felt very nostalgic. I had last used that turkey roaster back in 1964 when I cooked for our Company's first-anniversary Seminar.

As I washed the old roaster off, I felt like pinching myself to see if I was dreaming. It seemed like a lifetime ago, but it was only seventeen years. "We've come a long way, baby!" I told that old turkey roaster.

Our first headquarters was a five-hundred-square-foot storefront in Exchange Park, a large office building complex in Dallas. As I have said, we opened the doors on Friday, September 13, 1963, exactly one month to the day after my husband died. I had invested what I thought was a fortune ($5,000) in formulations, jars, and used office equipment.

Richard and I had great hopes for our Exchange Park location. The Exchange Bank occupied a major portion of the first floor of the building, and a number of national companies were tenants on the remaining floors. There were also several shops, including a coffee shop, drugstore, and a restaurant in the building's mall, which catered to the five thousand women who worked in the different offices. We figured we'd get lots of sales from that captive market. They'd go right by each morning on their way to work, and then they'd go right past us again on their way out every evening. And they did—they went right past us. In the morning, they were rushing to get to work on time, and in the evening, they were anxious to get home. The only advantage we had was that they did get coffee breaks twice a day. Before very long, we learned to give the fastest facials you've ever seen! We even learned to dry the masque quickly with an electric fan.

We had anticipated that it would be difficult to get women to stop in to learn about an unknown line of cosmetics. So many women will say, "I've been using Brand X for years, and I'm perfectly happy with it!" We needed something unusual to attract customers, and I thought of offering wigs.

In 1963, wigs were a new idea to American women, and they were the latest fad. I went to a wig school in Florida to learn all about them, and then we bought an inventory of good human-hair wigs. We were ready for our grand opening, and we all were nervous about it. If we didn't succeed, I knew I'd be back working for someone else for the rest of my life.

It was Richard who came up with the idea of a glamorous grand opening. We hired Renee of Paris, a wig stylist, to style any wigs purchased that day. And we hired a darling little model to serve champagne to the customers. This really didn't feel right to me, but I went along with it. And sure enough, who do you think the pretty model with the champagne attracted? The men in the building, not the women! But it wasn't a total flop. We did sell about a dozen wigs to the women who did come in, and Renee styled them all very elegantly. Naturally, the women who were blond bought brunette wigs—and the brunettes all wanted blond wigs.

We were very excited about those first-day sales until Monday morning! Then we learned that it's a terrible mistake to buy a wig that's noticeably different from your own hair. A wig should supplement a woman's wardrobe, and help her look good when she doesn't have time to style her hair. But we didn't know how important it was to teach our customers that, and we had sold them what they wanted. Well, of course, when they walked in the door, the first thing their husbands said was "Goldilocks! What in the world happened to you?" Men just don't appreciate drastic changes like that. Although we didn't have to accept returned wigs, we did on Monday morning.

After that, we were very careful to advise customers on the color of wigs they bought. And the wigs did serve as a drawing card, and attracted women who, many times, bought cosmetics. Our Beauty Consultants took wigs to shows, too. Since our main concern was our skin care products, the wigs weren't brought out until the facials were completed. But taking wigs to shows presented all kinds of problems. For one thing, a wig styled for one person can look all wrong on someone else. Therefore, the Consultants had to take several of those expensive wigs to every show. And if the wig wasn't handled carefully, a set could easily be ruined.

The wigs also took up a lot of space in our Exchange Park storefront. We stored the wigs and styled them in the back room, so that room was a mess, with hair dryers and curlers all over the place. We kept the front room decorated nicely, because that's where we worked with our customers. But that meant we had nowhere to store our cosmetics. Finally we rented basement storage, and that solved our space problem. But to get there, you had to go out in the mall, walk half a block, go down a long flight of stairs, and then walk another hundred yards in the basement to our small space. It amounted to being about two blocks away. Richard, who was in charge of all our bookkeeping then, also had the job of going down to storage to fill orders.

I always insisted that Richard dress like a businessman, although, even with his coat and tie, he still looked like a teenager. But he had lovely manners with the customers. Once a sale was made, he'd take the order very formally and say, "Yes, ma'am, I'll be right back." As soon as he started down the stairs, he would start peeling off his coat, and by the time he reached the door, he'd have his tie off. He'd run all the way to that storage area, and put the order together. Then he would put his tie and jacket back on, straighten his shoulders, and run back. By the time he walked into the showroom, he'd be just as dignified as you please, and he would hand the customer the merchandise as if he were delivering a silver platter.

He was running himself to death, up and down those steps. As our business grew, his administrative work grew, too. Finally, his older brother, Ben, came into the business, and the situation eased. Ben worked out of that basement storage area, and we called orders in to him.

In early 1965, Richard said, "I've had it. I'm sick and tired of these wigs. We've got to get rid of them." It *was* getting ridiculous. We figured it was taking about eight hours of a Consultant's time to sell a wig. First she had to bring the customer in to sell her and fit the wig and then she had to bring the customer back a second time to get the finished wig. It was time-consuming for everyone involved. Taking the wigs out of our line turned out to be a good decision. Our Consultants zeroed in on the cosmetics, and the next month our sales went up $20,000!

Well, both my sons were now in the business with me. Richard had given up his job as an insurance agent, and Ben had left his job as a welder. Needless to say, both sets of inlaws had tried desperately to talk them out of it: "How *can* you give up a good, solid career to go into *that* foolish business your mother is starting?"

By this time, another member of the family had entered the business—my daughter, Marylyn. I had visited Marylyn in Houston at Thanksgiving the first year and given her a beauty case when our business was just two months old. No training, no manual—just a beauty case. "Do something with this," I said. Of course, Marylyn had been using the products for years, and she loved them, so I really didn't have to tell her anything about them. Although she had children, and she was working alone in Houston, Marylyn began working toward becoming a Director, and she did a fine job. Later she did become a Director and kept that position for four years. Unfortunately, she had some problems with her back which made it necessary for her to leave the business. If she had been able to stay with us, she would be one of our top Directors today.

My first Beauty Consultants, all nine of them, were friends. There were other people I longed to recruit, but I had made a firm decision not to proselyte people working with other direct sales companies. My very first Consultant, Dalene White, had previously worked for my husband's company, and came with me because she felt so bad about his death. It was her way of being a good friend. Today, Dalene is one of our National Sales Directors, and her earnings in 1980 exceeded $200,000. Four of the original nine Consultants are still with the company, too. (Dalene and Helen McVoy became our very first "Mary Kay Millionaires," each having earned more than $1,000,000 in commissions!)

Some of those original Consultants have admitted that they just came in on a temporary basis. I was so enthusiastic, they couldn't say no! There were others, of course, who didn't join, and only watched to see how long it would take us to go broke. With hindsight, you can say, "Gee, they made a mistake." But back then, it didn't look like we really knew what we were doing. Everything was still experimental—we just did things by the golden rule.

The first decision we had to make when we set up the company was what our sales technique would be. I wanted to use some of the concepts of the party plan, but in a new way, with a small, intimate beauty show. I knew the best way for me to develop the sales presentation was to go out and give shows myself. But I soon learned that people didn't appreciate having the owner of the company there. "You *own* this company and you're at my house giving facials? Must be an awfully small company." And they figured that if the company was that small, the products couldn't be very good. So before long, I decided to stop giving shows, much as I loved to. From then on, I had to theorize about what would and wouldn't work, based on my own experience and on what the Consultants were telling me. Over a period of time, we did develop a sales presentation and a training program.

One of the things I concentrated on during that time was developing a training manual for Consultants. I worked very hard on it, and when I got the first one ready, I thought it was pretty impressive. It had five pages—and one of them was a "Welcome Letter"! Today, the Mary Kay training guide has more than one hundred pages, developed by our successful Directors sharing their knowledge.

We had a Basic Skin Care Set when we began, just as we do now—with Cleansing Cream, Magic Masque, Skin Freshener, Night Cream, and Day Radiance. The products were in little jars and bottles, and each Consultant had a set—and she'd pass around each jar for every woman there to use. That was before we really knew about sanitation. Nowadays, I'm aghast at the thought that we didn't know any better!

We always knew that the five items in the Basic Set all work together to help keep a woman's skin beautiful. But in the beginning, we would break the Basic, so if a woman wanted to buy just the Magic Masque, for instance, we'd sell it to her. The same was true if she wanted just the Cleansing Cream, or just the Skin Freshener. Then, a few months later, when she was contacted, she would say, "It didn't work for me." Well, breaking up the Basic Set that way was like giving you my recipe for chocolate cake but leaving out an important ingredient. It's just not going to be my cake. Because if you apply the masque by itself, without cleansing the face first and following with the Skin Freshener, it will probably have a drying effect. The products in the Basic Set complement each other. Somebody once referred to the whole skin care process as a prescription in five jars, and that's a pretty good description. So we finally came to the conclusion that we would not break the Basic Set. We preferred to face the customer's ire in the beginning than to have her fail to get results.

In the beginning, we even broke the Day Radiance. It comes in skin tones, and also in yellow, to dab on any little red spots or blotches you might have. Well, if a Consultant was holding a Show where there were three people who wanted just a little bit of yellow Day Radiance, the Consultant would take a knife and waxed paper and divide that into three parts for them, and then let them draw to see who got the box! I can't *believe* we did that, but we did.

Our first inventory included the Basic Set and five more items—rouge, lip and eye palette, mascara, and eyebrow pencil—for the total line of ten products. I remember that we stored our entire Mary Kay inventory on a $9.95 steel shelving unit from Sears on our first day. Today, we have approximately forty products in our line, excluding shade variations, and the average Consultant probably has more inventory than the whole company did when we opened!

We thought the products were wonderful when we started Mary Kay, but we knew we could make them even better. Now, we invest millions in research to continue to improve and refine every product in the line. Today, there are formulas for virtually every skin type because, as I said, personalizing the beauty process is our specialty. We teach women exactly how to use our products because we want them to get the best possible results.

In the beginning, our products were made by a private

Dallas manufacturing company. I chose a company run by a man with an excellent reputation in the cosmetic field. We knew it was essential to find someone who was ethical and reliable. I took the formulations to this company, and the owner just turned the whole thing over to his son. I'm sure he thought he'd never see *us* again after this first small order. I suppose that, like everyone else, he gave us little hope. But we did come back with another order and another and a few years later we were in a position to have his son come and head our own manufacturing division.

Richard, Ben, and I put in sixteen- and eighteen-hour workdays when we first started the business, staying after closing time to do anything that had to be done. We would fill and pack orders, and sometimes we'd be in that basement storage area until two in the morning writing and mimeographing our newsletters. But our hard work paid off. During our first three and a half months in business, we had $34,000 in sales, and showed a small profit. The first calendar year, we had $198,000 in wholesale sales. At the end of the second year, we had reached $800,000 in sales.

We had been in business only a year and we were expanding so rapidly that we needed new offices. We moved to 1220 Majesty Drive. Now we had three offices, one for me and one each for Richard and Ben, a training room, and a huge warehouse—five thousand square feet of space in all! It seemed like the Grand Canyon to us!

On September 13, 1964, we held our first major meeting— and we called it "Seminar." We couldn't afford to rent space in a hotel, so we held it in the warehouse of the new Majesty Drive location. I still remember how enthusiastic we all were—and how hard we worked to save money! We decorated the warehouse with crepe paper and balloons, so that it would look festive. Our menu was simple, chicken with Jalapeño dressing and a Jell-O salad. The little paper plates we used were flimsy, and you couldn't have cut a thing on them, so I boned all the chicken for two hundred people. I cooked the chicken and dressing in advance and froze it, and then the old turkey roaster was used to heat it. I also made up a huge orange Jell-O salad with all kinds of goodies in it. But I didn't stop to consider that it was September, and Texas isn't all that cool in September. That Jell-O melted all over the place! But people sat, holding their plates on their laps, and doing the best they could, and everyone proclaimed it a great Seminar. One of the Directors from Tyler, Texas, Ellen Notley, baked a big cake that said, Happy First Anniversary! and a three-piece band entertained.

It *was* a happy anniversary for us—two hundred of us by the end of that first year. After dinner, I acted as master of ceremonies and we had our first annual awards night! It was very modest compared to what we do now, but we were all thrilled. Seminar is still a big event here at Mary Kay, and later on I want to tell you what it has grown into today.

Not long ago, I ran across a speech I gave at one of those early Seminars. I've kept a copy of every speech I've ever made, and sometimes I go back and refer to material from old speeches. I've used this particular speech several times. The original copy says, "And next year, we expect to have three thousand people in our sales force!" I remember writing that. Richard told me that was the projected figure, but at the time I just thought, "Goodness! Imagine having three thousand people!" I used this page of this particular speech the next year too, and the three thousand was scratched out. The number had grown to eleven thousand. Then it was scratched out again a couple of years later, and the figure became an unbelievable forty thousand. Over the years, that number has just kept growing. Today, we have more than 100,000 Beauty Consultants representing Mary Kay. We have come a long way since those early years.

By the way, the old turkey roaster has officially been retired from the business world. But I want you to know, it still cooks a terrific Thanksgiving turkey!

❦ 5 ❦

That Mary Kay Enthusiasm

For some reason, singing seems to unite people. Remember in high school and in college, when you sang those "Rah rah rah—for our team" songs? That group spirit we all experienced is known as *esprit de corps.*

When I worked for Stanley Home Products, the company had a number of songs which were always sung before and during our sales meetings, and it really helped to build *esprit de corps.* After I left Stanley and joined a company called World Gift, I found a real lack of that spirit. In fact, they were kind of a gruff group of people at first. So, I introduced a song contest, and the people came up with dozens of World Gift songs. I watched those songs change the temperament of the whole sales force.

When we started this company, I decided to have a Mary Kay song contest. We would take the songs we thought were best, play them at Seminar, and the people would sing them. The ones that seemed most acceptable would be awarded prizes.

Now, the secret of a well-received song is to write your own words to a well-known tune. So somebody wrote a song to the tune of an old and much-loved hymn. "I've Got That Mary Kay Enthusiasm" instantly became the song most accepted by our sales force. And today, "That Mary Kay Enthusiasm" is so much a part of our company that it is sung every-where. Even though the melody is a hymn, certainly no irreverence is intended on the part of our people.

Our Consultants and Directors sing dozens of Mary Kay songs. Another very popular one is, "If You Want to Be a Di-rector, Clap Your Hands." It ends with, "If you want to be a Director, you've got to be a 'perfecter,' so do all three, clap your hands, stomp your feet, and yell *hooray*." Again, it's a catchy tune that just about everybody knows. It's invariably sung at guest nights, and you can always spot the guests. They're the ones who don't participate. They just stand there wondering, "What's happening?" But the strange thing is that if the same songs are sung again at the *end* of guest night, you find very few people who aren't singing. And by the third meeting, *everyone* joins in the singing!

Those songs really do build *esprit de corps,* and they play an important part in our sales meetings. Most of our sales meetings are held on Monday mornings. Monday, to the aver-age woman, means "a new beginning." Of course, to many people Monday signals the end of a carefree weekend and has come to be known as "blue Monday." Whatever the case, Monday morning sales meetings with their inspiration, moti-vation, and enthusiastic songs get the new week started off in "high gear"!

This is why I think that the best time of the week for a sales meeting is Monday morning. Many of our Directors also have a Monday evening meeting for those people who have nine-to-five jobs and sell Mary Kay on a part-time basis. Mon-day is a new week and even if last week was not good for *you,* it *was* good for someone else! We often say, "If you had a bad week—*you* need the sales meeting. If you had a *good* week, the sales meeting needs *you!*" When a Consultant leaves a sales meeting all excited, she has an entire week to let that excite-ment work for her, instead of a partial one if the sales meeting is held later in the week.

Just as Monday morning meetings generate enthusiasm, I

believe a mother can generate morning enthusiasm in her family. If she gets up all grumpy, the chances are the whole family will leave the house with the same attitude that day. Even though a mother might not feel like it, she should make every effort to smile and say a cheery "Good morning, how are you this morning?" Before long, even if she didn't *feel* cheerful to start with, she'll feel better and the rest of the family will be in a happier mood, too. I really believe that if you *act* enthusiastic, you will *become* enthusiastic! Not just for a day but for a lifetime!

One of the best examples I ever saw of making yourself enthusiastic happened several years ago, when we had engaged a prominent person to come and speak to us. His flight was delayed, so it was necessary to keep improvising the program until he arrived. Finally, I was given the signal that he was there. He had come rushing in and was waiting offstage.

Since I was the emcee, I had a whole page of typewritten accolades for him, and I began enthusiastically giving his introduction. While I was doing this, with my peripheral vision I could see him offstage—beating his chest and jumping up and down, for all the world looking like a gorilla! I thought, "My goodness. Here I am saying all these wonderful things about this man, and *he* has just 'flipped'!" I had never seen *anyone* act so strangely.

When I finished the introduction, he came running out, and gave a *fantastic* speech. It was really motivating! Afterward, sitting next to him at lunch, I said, "You know, you almost scared me to death. What in the world were you *doing* back there, jumping up and down and beating on your chest like that?"

"Well, Mary Kay," he said, "my job is motivation. And some days I just don't feel like it. This was one of them! I've really had a hectic time with my flight being delayed this morning. But I knew you were expecting me to be an enthusiastic, vibrant, exciting speaker. I just couldn't 'rain on your parade,' especially when I saw all those excited people in the audience. I had to turn myself on. And I've found that if I just churn up my blood with some exercise and chest beating, I feel much better. So that's what I was doing."

You *can* do things to make yourself enthusiastic. But don't you also know some people who are just naturally enthusiastic and expressive, and others who aren't? It's interesting to note that the word *enthusiasm* comes from a Greek word meaning "God within." Enthusiasm is a great advantage in anything you do—and certainly in sales. I'm sure my own enthusiasm was my number-one asset when I first got into sales.

I was a very young housewife when I learned what the gift of enthusiasm could accomplish. One day, a lady came to my door selling the Child Psychology Bookshelf. It was a series of books for children. If you had a problem with your child, you simply looked up the problem in the back of the book, and there was a story to tie in with it. All the stories included very good morals, and whatever the problem was, there was a story to fit the situation. As a young mother trying to teach her children the difference between right and wrong, I just thought those were the best books I'd ever seen! When the saleslady told me what the books cost, I almost cried. I just couldn't afford them. Sensing my interest, she let me keep them over the weekend, and I read every page. When she came by to pick them up, I was heartbroken. I told her I was going to save my money, and one day I would buy those books, because they were the best I'd ever seen.

When she saw how excited I was she said, "I'll tell you what, Mary Kay, if you sell ten sets of books for me, I'll give you a set." Well, that was just wonderful! I started calling my friends, and the parents of my beginner Sunday School students at Tabernacle Baptist Church. I didn't even have any books to show them—I just had my enthusiasm.

In a day and a half, I sold ten sets of books. I just told people these were the best books I'd ever seen. I was so excited, they got excited, too. When the saleslady, Ida Blake, came back, she couldn't believe it! I had customers lined up so all she had to do was go to their homes and have them sign the papers. She came back and she was amazed. She couldn't get over it. "How did you *do* it?" she asked me.

I didn't know what I had done. I had no idea those books were hard to sell. She gave me my set of books and said, "Look, I want you to work for me." She asked if I had a car. I answered, "Yes, we do, but I don't know how to drive." We did have a ramshackle old car that my husband drove to his job at the service station every morning and to his musical engagements at night. Ida told me to be sure he left the car the next day. She came early in the morning, and we left in my car. She was going to teach me how to sell books!

She drove us out to a suburb, and we knocked on doors all day long! By the end of that day, I was exhausted. I had never been so tired in my life. We didn't make a single sale. Not one person was even remotely interested. I couldn't get over it. I had sold ten sets in a day and a half, and I couldn't understand why she was having so much trouble. I hadn't realized the power of my enthusiasm.

At 5:00 P.M., Ida got in on the passenger's side of the car and announced, "You're driving home."

"But I don't know how to drive."

Well, she figured if I was going to be a saleswoman, I had to know how to drive. "You're going to learn right now," she said. She gave me one quick lesson, and off we went—right into the Houston rush hour, with its bumper-to-bumper traffic. I practically stripped the gears, but we did get home. The next day, I guess I let my enthusiasm for my new skill as a driver get the best of me. I drove down to my mother's restaurant—very proud of myself—and knocked down two of the three posts that held up the porch above the sidewalk. The posts fell right on top of the car and just about ruined it!

However, I was learning how to drive, and I had my first sales job, thanks to Ida Blake. During the next nine months, I sold $25,000 worth of books. At a 30 to 40 percent commission, I was making good money. But I finally decided to quit. I had sold so many sets to my friends, and the next time I would see them, they'd be unhappy with me. It was not because the books weren't good—they were. But they blamed me because my enthusiasm had led them to buy the books, and then they didn't *use* them. Well, what good were the books if they were never read? But to this day, I still think those books were great!

I had one other sales experience before I went to work for Stanley. Shortly after I stopped selling the Child Psychology Bookshelf, my husband lost his job at the filling station and went to work selling cookware. We worked as a team, selling special sets of alloy cookware—pressure cookers, double fry-pans, those kinds of things. The selling was based on actual demonstrations, and that's where I came in. I would purchase the food, prepare it during the day, and on the evening of the demonstration, we would bring everything to the prospect's home and put on a dinner party. The menu was always the same: green beans, ham, sweet potatoes, and a cake. It was supposed to look like child's play, and since I put a lot of time into purchasing the finest cut of ham and the tenderest green beans and sweet potatoes available and carefully preparing them and the cake batter in advance, it looked easy. My husband would give the sales presentation to several couples in the living room, and I would be back in the kitchen with that pressure cooker and double fry-pan, cooking the meal.

In reality, it was I who made the sales, because the wives would invariably come out in the kitchen and ask me questions like "Is it really as easy as it looks?" And of course, I would answer that the cookware was wonderful (it really was!).

Though my husband took the orders, the selling really happened in the kitchen. It was food we couldn't afford to buy for ourselves. And that same menu was our dinner every night if there was any food left over after the demonstration dinner. If our prospective customers ate it all, we just didn't eat that night.

We finally quit. It was during the Depression and most people simply couldn't afford new cookware. Selling it took what I considered a "hard sell," and I've never been very good at that.

At Mary Kay Cosmetics, we discourage aggressive selling. We prefer to *teach* skin care, and simply express our enthusiasm for our product. We don't look for people who want to hard sell, but for people who like to teach. As a result, hundreds of former teachers and nurses are part of our sales force. They find they can earn as much as, or in many cases more than, they had been earning, and being a Beauty Consultant is to them more interesting and exciting.

I think most women appreciate our low-key presentation. Sometimes we refer to it as "polite persuasion." We present our skin care line in an enthusiastic, knowledgeable way, and most of us feel it simply sells itself. We frequently receive letters from customers and hostesses complimenting our Consultants on their polite and professional presentations.

This kind of selling ensures customer loyalty and enthusiasm for our products, too. Because we aren't aggressive, customers trust us in a way they wouldn't trust a company that used pressure to sell. I remember one most unusual letter from a woman whose husband had come home one day and said, "Honey, start packing. My company is moving me to Venezuela for a year. We leave in three days."

She wrote, "In a matter of a week we were here in Venezuela. And we no sooner arrived than I found I had only about a three-week supply of my Mary Kay Cosmetics. I panicked, because I cannot do without those products."

So she had made a list of what she used and the colors she needed—and *she enclosed a signed, blank check* and asked us to send her a year's supply!

I'm sure her husband would have been extremely upset about his wife sending a signed, blank check through the mail to a company—had he known about it. I looked at that letter and thought, "It's a good thing this is an honest company!"

Then I carefully figured out what *I* would need if I were going to be in Venezuela for a year. Based on my own personal usage, I completed that order for her, filled out the check, and saw to it that the shipment got off that afternoon. Needless to say, I was very touched to think that somebody wanted our products so much that she would send a signed, blank check to avoid delay.

It's not unusual for a customer's husband to be enthusiastic about our products, too. Not long ago, the receptionist buzzed me and said, "Mary Kay, there's a man on the line who is asking to speak to the 'real thing'—if there is one."

"What does he want?"

"He won't say. He said he'll only talk to the 'real thing.' "

I told her to put him on, and I have *never* heard a man talk so fast! I think he was afraid I would hang up. He said, "Mary Kay, I called to thank you for saving my marriage."

Since I didn't know this man, I couldn't imagine how I might have saved his marriage. Before I could interrupt, he went right on, "My wife and I have been married for eight years, and when we were first married, she looked like something right out of *Vogue* magazine. She had every hair in place, a beautiful face and figure, and I loved her very much. Then she became pregnant, and it was one of those pregnancies that make a woman sick the entire nine months. She lost all interest in her appearance. And then we had a second child, one right after the other."

He was talking so fast I didn't have a chance to say a word.

"Well," he went on, "it got to the point that when I left in the morning there she was—with one kid hanging onto her dirty housecoat, and another kid screaming in her arms. Her hair wasn't combed and her face was never made up. When I came home at night, the only thing that had changed was that it was worse! About two months ago, she went to a Mary Kay Beauty Show, and she bought twenty-eight dollars worth of that stuff." I could tell that this amount sounded like the national debt to him.

"But," he said, "that girl who sold it to her really did a good job! My wife probably figured I'd be mad at her for spending twenty-eight dollars on cosmetics, so when she got home she fixed her face. And as soon as she made up her face, she had to do her hair and then she got dressed. When I got home that night, she looked *terrific!* It had been so long since I had seen her looking that way that I had forgotten how she could look. And the best part is that every morning now when she gets up, she fixes her face and her hair again, and gets dressed. Besides that, she's lost twelve pounds and I've got my old girl back. I've fallen in love with her all over again and it's all your fault!"

Then he hung up. Those were his last words—"It's all your fault." I never *did* get a chance to ask him who he was, or who the Beauty Consultant was who did such a great job. But I went immediately into the sales meeting being held that day and told them what had happened. Then I said, "How do you know it wasn't *you* who performed this little miracle?" And I still tell that story, because that's probably happened a million times but very few men would actually take the time to telephone.

Sometimes my own enthusiasm for Mary Kay products makes a sale when I'm not even thinking about making a sale. It can happen at the oddest times. One interesting incident happened to me and my late husband, Mel, on our delayed honeymoon trip to Rome in 1966. We were sitting at one of those long tables in an open-air restaurant near the Colosseum, where everyone is seated side by side. Mel was saying, "Where *are* all those beautiful women Europe is so famous for? I haven't seen *any* beautiful women on this trip."

Just then, a gorgeous woman walked in—tall, thin, and stately. She had beautiful black hair and an ivory complexion, and she was very well dressed. We both decided she must be an Italian countess.

Sure enough, the waiter seated her next to Mel, and her husband next to me. A few minutes later, Mel took out a pack of cigarettes, and the man asked if he might have one. He explained that they had been in Europe for six weeks and he hadn't been able to get any American cigarettes. Mel graciously gave him the pack, and the man said, "Thank you. I will treasure these."

After that, they began talking, and the man asked Mel what business he was in. Mel told him, "I'm in a gift business, and my wife is in the cosmetic business."

The woman immediately became very interested. "Cosmetics? What kind?"

"Mary Kay Cosmetics," I answered. "You probably have never heard about us. We're a small company in Texas, just a little more than two years old." Then, before I knew it, I was enthusiastically telling her about our products. That evening, the purse I was carrying was so small that it wouldn't even hold a lip and eye palette, so I had *nothing* to show her. But by the time we had finished dinner, she was writing out a check for one of *everything* in our line! She explained that she would be back home in Acapulco in three months and she asked if I would have the items sent to her by then. My enthusiasm about our products had excited her so much, she wanted to try *everything!*

After receiving the products, she became even more excited about them. She kept sending orders for three to six complete collections *every month.* I was amazed, because the import duty in Mexico is almost 100 percent, so a collection was costing twice the United States price. Finally, I wrote her and asked what in the world she was doing with all the cosmetics she had ordered. She explained that her friends kept asking her what she was using—she looked so radiant—and she had been giving them facials and presenting them with the products as gifts.

Enthusiasm does spread like that. We have an expression at Mary Kay, "The speed of the leader is the speed of the gang." Just as a salesperson or a satisfied customer can generate enthusiasm in someone else, one person can also generate it in a whole group. The best way to do it is by example. If a

Director is enthusiastic, the Consultants in her unit will be enthusiastic. Our Directors set a wonderful example for their Consultants to follow. It is my feeling that each of them is "Mary Kay" to her people. The Consultants, in turn are "Mary Kay" to their customers.

I am thankful that I have been blessed with natural enthusiasm. I'm sure my enthusiasm is responsible for my high energy level. Even after all these years in business, no matter how exhausted I might be late at night, in the morning I wake up with renewed enthusiasm. I love what I do, and each day presents new opportunities to love and encourage each working woman—to success!

I like what Ralph Waldo Emerson said: "Nothing great was ever achieved without enthusiasm." And just think, he didn't even *know* about Mary Kay enthusiasm!

6

Put on a Happy Face

For about a year after my divorce from my first husband, I felt that I had failed as a woman, as a wife, as a person. I just couldn't accept the fact that our marriage had failed. Being in such a terrible frame of mind caused me to have physical symptoms that several doctors diagnosed as rheumatoid arthritis. Finally, the doctors at the renowned Scott and White Memorial Hospital in Temple, Texas, told me it was progressing so rapidly that within a matter of months I would be a hopeless cripple.

I couldn't bear the idea of having to return home and have my mother support me—and my three children. She had worked so hard all her life, and was still working hard. The prospect was just unthinkable!

I worked for Stanley Home Products at the time, and since I had a family to support and I only made $10 or $12 a party, I had to give three Stanley parties a day just to make ends meet. I realized that in order to be successful, I had to leave my personal problems at home. I decided that no matter how I felt, I would go in there with a smile. And, as I succeeded in selling, my health kept getting better, until finally all the symptoms of rheumatoid arthritis disappeared. Actually, in retrospect, I think the physical symptoms were induced by my extreme emotional stress. However, even as my physical health improved, the doctors continued to insist that I was simply in a remission and that I could be sure the arthritis would return. But all these years later—and it never has!

The funny thing about putting on a happy face is that if you do it again and again, pretty soon that happy face is there to stay. It becomes *the real you.* I discovered that by maintaining a cheerful attitude during those three Stanley parties every day. One by one, my problems seemed to go away. But if I had allowed myself to be depressed, I wouldn't have done a good job selling, and my problems would have compounded.

It has always been my philosophy that a salesperson should never discuss personal problems with customers. I suggest that our Consultants mentally "turn off their problems" before they go to a Show. When people ask, "How are you?" they don't *really* want to know! They don't care that your husband has lost his job, your children have chicken pox, or your water heater just broke down. Don't inflict your troubles on them. If you do, it creates a negative atmosphere that can just destroy rapport. It's best to never let anyone know you have a problem. I've always tried not to. When I came through the door, little did anyone know I had left a myriad of problems at home. I just put on my happy face. I know some people thought of me as Pollyanna. Nobody suspected that behind my big smile I did, indeed, have all sorts of troubles.

I suggest to our Consultants that no matter how bad they might feel before a Beauty Show, they must always go in enthusiastically. When the hostess says, "Hello, how are you?" the Consultant must respond, "Wonderful! And how are you?"—even if she has to say it through clenched teeth! She must act enthusiastic and happy all through that Show. If she does a good job, and comes out with a $200 Show, she *will* be enthusiastic and happy.

It's important to realize that nobody is highly motivated *every* day. There are days when even the most enthusiastic person will wake up feeling depressed. And yes, I have days when I wake up and just don't feel "with it." I might be tired, or perhaps there's something on my schedule that I'm not looking forward to doing. Those are the times when I work to generate enthusiasm. Somebody once said, "A man is about as happy as he makes up his mind to be," and I believe that!

Then, too, I'm continually reading good motivational books and I also listen to motivational tapes while I'm dressing in the morning, and while I'm driving back and forth to the office. It's a wonderful way to keep from "wasting" that time.

Singing seems to cheer people up, too. I've told you about the songs we sing at Mary Kay get-togethers. Some people have criticized us for this, because they think the songs are silly. But we have found that when people are in a negative frame of mind, those songs have a wonderful effect on them. I believe that's the same reason churches begin their services with hymns. I remember as a young mother driving to church with three small children squabbling in the back seat. Sometimes I felt I had lost my religion by the time I got there! I was in no mood to be in church, but after I'd sung two or three hymns, I felt a lot better, and I was ready to absorb my pastor's message.

At the beginning of our sales meetings, we have what we call a "Crow Period." This is a time when Consultants tell about their successes during the past week. We encourage them to "crow." And after one person is through, someone else will jump up enthusiastically and tell the group about something wonderful that happened to her. After hearing a couple of dozen people talk about how well they've done, even if you've had a bad week, you begin to think, "If they can do it, I can do it, too!" A happy face and a happy attitude is always an inspiration to others.

Of course, there are times when it takes a great deal of effort to put on a happy face. My husband, Mel, passed away on Monday, July 7, 1980. On Tuesday night, all our staff and Directors and Consultants would be leaving Dallas for St. Louis, where 7,500 Directors and Consultants were gathering from throughout the midwest for a meeting.

All of those people dearly loved Mel. The funeral had to be held Tuesday afternoon so they could attend it. Because of Mel's illness and then death, I had not planned to go. You can understand, I was grief-stricken, and these meetings are supposed to be joyful, inspirational times. I knew that many women there were spending a good deal of money to travel to that Jamboree, and I felt an obligation not to let them down. I went on Friday, and when I got there I made certain to generate a positive attitude for everybody there. I went out in front of a large audience, and I did my best to project the happiness I felt for them, rather than the sorrow I felt for myself. I knew my mood would project to everyone there, and I wanted them to have a positive experience.

I kept thinking of Jackie Kennedy Onassis, and how courageous she was when her husband was assassinated. The whole world praised her for her courage. She wouldn't allow herself the luxury of breaking down, and her strength had a tremendous impact on many other people. Later, when they faced tragedies in their own lives, they remembered how she had kept her head up, not crying in public, and they knew that they could do it, too. In my own small way, I was trying to do the same thing at our Jamboree. Since then, I've received countless letters from women telling me that the fact that I was able to put on a happy face during my grief has inspired them to do the same thing when they've suffered a tragedy in their own lives.

Life has its sad moments, but living must always go on. Just a few days before our 1978 Seminar, another tragedy occurred. One of our most beautiful and talented National Sales Directors, Sue Vickers, was kidnapped in the parking lot of a Dallas shopping center and murdered. Sue was known in our company as "Miss Enthusiasm," and her warmth and "Go-Give" spirit were an inspiration to everyone who knew her. Her death was heartbreaking.

Sue was scheduled to give a speech at Seminar. Among her notes for the speech, she had written:

Be Somebody—Be Great.
I Can Do All Things Through Christ Who Strengthens Me.
Do Big Things—Don't Give Up!
Be an Inspiration to Others!
What the World Needs Is a Word of Good Cheer!
Enthusiasm! Love! And Laughter!

These thoughts show the kind of person Sue was. Her senseless death was a great loss to me personally, as well as to everyone else who knew her. But we put on our happy faces, dedicated the Seminar to Sue, and it went on as scheduled. I'm sure that's the way Sue would have wanted it.

It's easy to smile and be enthusiastic when everything is going along perfectly in your life. Under ideal circumstances, anyone can project cheerfulness. But the real test of a champion is to be able to put on a happy face when deep down you're suffering over a serious personal problem.

One such champion is Rena Tarbet. Rena is a mother of three, in her late thirties, and she's on her way to being a National Sales Director. She's had so much success with Mary Kay, making $8,000 or $10,000 a month, that her husband has been able to quit a job he disliked and work in a children's home. So now they're both doing work they love. Rena is so positive and cheerful you would never know that she's had two mastectomies in the past five years. She's started reconstruction surgery, and she *knows* she'll be okay.

Rena has an attitude that is an inspiration to everyone. She's so enthusiastic! She loves life; she loves her work; and she isn't letting illness stop her. She has an inspiring story about something that happened while she was waiting to be tested at M. D. Anderson Hospital and Tumor Research Institute at Houston. She had waited all day, and she was next, when the head nurse announced to everyone that the doctor would be unable to see anybody else until the next afternoon. Rena had a Mary Kay workshop to conduct the next day. So she went up to the physician and told him she had to be in Dallas the following afternoon.

"Is there any reason why you couldn't see just one more patient today, doctor?" she asked. He thought about it for a minute, and because of her smiling attitude, consented to her request.

When she told me about it, she beamed. "I used the same selling technique you taught me," she said, "where we ask a woman, 'Is there any reason why you couldn't be a hostess for a Beauty Show?'"

After her workshop, she told me what they had found. She would probably have to receive chemotherapy and radiation treatments for the next eighteen months. It's likely she'll lose all her hair. But when I talked to her about it, she just smiled and said, "Guess I'll have to get myself a really pretty wig, Mary Kay."

As I listened to Rena talk so positively, I admired her serene and cheerful expression. I had to fight to hold back my own tears, and it took everything I had to "put on a happy face." Yet, as I looked at Rena's happy face, I knew I could do no less. At a recent meeting, she told the audience that her spirits were high and her determination was unyielding. She shared with us a quote from Montaigne's *Essays*: "The value of life lies not in the length of days but in the use we make of them. A man may live long yet get little from life. Whether you find satisfaction in life depends not on your tale of years but on your will."

Rena had shared her passion for life with us and now, as I looked at her, I was filled with pride. I knew she had truly discovered the meaning of life, complete with its joys and sorrows. I gave her a big hug and, thankfully, only my happy emotions came pouring out.

7

God First, Family Second, Career Third

Over the years, I have found that if you have your life in the proper perspective, with God first, your family second, and your career third, everything seems to work out. I truly believe that the growth and success of Mary Kay Cosmetics has come about because the first thing we did was to take God as our partner. If we had not done that, I don't believe we would be where we are today. I believe He has blessed us because our motivation is right. He knows I want women to become the beautiful creatures He created—to *use* the wonderful God-given talents that lie within each of us.

I've found that when you just let go and place yourself in God's hands, everything in your life goes right. When you try to do everything alone, and rely just on yourself, you begin to make errors in your life.

Here at Mary Kay, I don't think we are as smart as the balance sheets would show. Nobody can know in advance what's going to happen several years down the road. Now, Richard is brilliant; he's outstanding at planning; and he's recognized today as one of the young financial geniuses on the American scene. But I just don't feel we're *that* brilliant. I believe God has helped us, because it seems as though everything we attempt just works out. I can't begin to tell you how many times we've needed something and sometimes before I can even ask, it's delivered to our door.

Our experience with hexachlorophene is a good example. This was an ingredient everyone felt was just wonderful, and it was in our body lotion. Well, we decided to remove it, and a very short time after that, the Food and Drug Administration came out and declared that hexachlorophene could not be used. We had to destroy about nineteen thousand bottles, but that was nothing compared to what might have happened. If we hadn't already stopped using hexachlorophene, we might have had hundreds of thousands of bottles out!

Now, Richard's reaction to this miraculous timing is, "Why, our scientists knew these things were going to happen, so they acted accordingly." But *nobody* knows what the FDA is going to do from one day to the next. You might hear rumors that such and such is going to happen, and maybe our scientists did. Perhaps there was talk that hexachlorophene was on the questionable list. But whatever the reason was, we had removed that chemical by the time the FDA issued their edict, and we avoided any problems.

This is just an example; there are so *many* decisions I feel we've been helped with. You know, you don't just make big decisions in a company. Sometimes it's the little, daily decisions, the ones you make by the hour, that mean the difference between success and failure. And I feel that God has had His protective arm around us and has guided us to make the right decision.

Although I believe that God has been instrumental in the growth of our business, I'm careful to remember that we are a business and that I must avoid "preaching" to our people. As a company with more than 100,000 people, we have members of every denomination affiliated with us; Presbyterians, Lutherans, Seventh-Day Adventists, Catholics, Jews, Jehovah's Witnesses, Buddhists, and Moslems. Just about every faith is represented in our company. Because of our company philosophy—God first, family second, job third—we seem to draw people of many faiths who agree that God and family should be preeminent in their lives. I never try to impose my personal religious beliefs on our people. I do, however, let it be known that God is a very important part of my own life.

I am also quite vocal about my belief in strong family ties. I stress that no matter how successful you are in your career, if you lose your family in the process of attaining that success, then you've failed. Money is not worth sacrificing your family. A career is a means to an end—a means by which you can provide comforts and security for the family. But what you accomplish in your career is not an end in itself. Unfortunately, some people get so buried in their work that they lose sight of what's really important in life.

When I first started supporting my family as a Stanley dealer, I only had room for three things in my life—God, my family, and my career. I had no social life at all. My whole life was geared to my three children, my work, and my church. I didn't know what it was like to take in a show or have dinner out with a friend. I was making $10 or $12 in commissions on each Stanley party, so I had to give three parties a day. And if I didn't sell, the children and I had no income.

My entire day was planned around the children's schedule. I got up at five so I could do my housework before they were up. Then I gave them a good breakfast and got them off to school. After they were gone, I left too—for my first party. I'd have another party in the early afternoon, and then I would make sure to be home to greet them when they got home from school. I gave them their supper and got them ready for bed, and then at seven I'd leave for my evening party. The baby-sitter would have them asleep long before I got back. It worked out fine. I was able to "have my cake and eat it too," because I was a working mother but I still had plenty of time with my children. I thanked God for my high energy level!

One of the things I was able to do for the children was

take them to the Gulf for summer vacations. We stayed in a beachfront room at the Galvez Hotel in Galveston, which is fifty miles from Houston. I would take them down to the beach in the morning and stay as long as I could without getting sunburned, and then I would go upstairs to our room. I would sit at the window and read a book and at the same time keep an eye on them. At lunch, I'd take them to get a hot dog or sandwich, and after they had eaten they would go back and play again, and I would go back to the window. Actually, the beach was not what I would have selected for myself, because with my fair skin I can't take very much sun. So my whole vacation was spent watching the children enjoy themselves.

Those two weeks in Galveston were the only time I didn't work. The rest of the year, my life was strictly God, family, and work, work, work. Recently I heard Dr. Joyce Brothers say that it's not all bad to be a workaholic; that it really just means you are totally committed. I would like to think she's right, because I certainly would have fallen into that category.

It was necessary for me to work every night in order to make ends meet. But, thanks to Richard, some of the neighbors didn't take too kindly to my late hours. By the time we moved to Dallas, I was making a good living and we had moved into a nice neighborhood. We had a two-story brick house with a little front porch and a large tree on the front lawn. By that time, I also had a housekeeper who was supposed to put the children to bed after I left. But apparently she would tuck them in and then go to her room. At any rate, Richard would wait until the house was quiet and climb down from the little balcony adjoining his room to the tree and climb down that, and he would sit on the curb waiting for his mother to come home.

He loves to tell this story now: "Mary Kay never could understand why the neighbors didn't like her. They would see me sitting on that curb and ask, 'Where's your Mother?' and I would say, 'She's at a party.'" Never mentioning that the "party" was a Stanley party—and my work!

Although I worked long, hard hours while the children were growing up, I arranged my work so I was there when they needed me. I made myself available to help with their homework, and they knew I would always lend an ear to discuss any problems they might have. One of the nicest things about my flexible hours was that I could always be home to give my tender, loving care if one of the children was ill. There was very little I ever let interfere with my work—except my family.

Employers need to understand that these *are* a woman's priorities. I've seen women with nine-to-five jobs come to work when they had a very sick child at home. In my opinion, their employers would have been better off to tell them to stay home and take care of the child. There's just no way a mother can keep her mind on her work when she's worried about a sick child.

My husband, Mel, was seriously ill with cancer for seven weeks before he died. For the first two weeks after we discovered his illness, we didn't really know whether it was terminal. But I sent a message to my office that I would not be in until Mel was better. I knew they all understood how I feel about family coming before business. And for those seven weeks, I didn't go to the office a single day. The office sent my paperwork home to me every day, and when Mel was sleeping, I would go to my desk and do whatever seemed really urgent.

Before this happened, I had been looking forward to giving a speech to the General Federation of Women's Clubs that was meeting in St. Louis in June of 1980. The speech had been arranged a year in advance, and there would be several thousand women attending from all over the country. I was excited about having the chance to share the Mary Kay philosophy with so many women. But I would have had to leave Mel for two days, and I just couldn't do that. So Dalene White, one of our National Sales Directors, went to St. Louis in my place and did an excellent job representing our company.

I'm aware that most companies expect their employees to put their jobs in first place in their lives. Yes, I know that a person can become so wrapped up in his or her work that the family is neglected. But I don't see how anyone could expect work to come before family in a time of real need.

I'm told that it's unusual for a company to encourage people to put family before career, but we've been doing that ever since we started our business. We back up our philosophy by doing things to show our employees that we care about their families.

We encourage our employees to put their families ahead of their work, and we've never had a problem with it. I believe that if other companies kept our priorities, they would benefit.

As I have said, throughout the years I've found that when you put God first, your family second, and your career third, everything seems to work out. Out of that order, nothing much seems to work. When you get to the bottom line, it doesn't matter how much money you've made, how big your house is, or how many cars you own. Nothing matters on that day when God calls you except your relationship with Jesus Christ. Each of us will come to that day—and if our lives aren't right, they were wasted!

$\backsim 8 \backsim$

The Many Hats
of the Working Woman

When a man goes to work in the morning, he kisses his wife and children good-bye, and he's off and running.

From the time he gets up, the average man doesn't have to lift a finger for anyone but himself. He showers, shaves, puts on the clothes his wife has laundered, and eats the breakfast his wife has prepared. Then he puts on his hat, says, "Good-bye, honey, have a nice day," and out he goes.

As he leaves the house, he doesn't have to think about a single thing but his career. He has no concern whatsoever about making the bed he slept in, or cleaning up the bathroom he just left in disarray, or planning dinner for that night, or taking the clothes he wore yesterday to the cleaners. He doesn't worry about who is going to scrub the kitchen floor, or vacuum, or dust the house, or any of the other countless jobs that have to be done. He simply puts on his *one* hat and goes to work!

His wife doesn't have it quite so easy, especially if she has a career, too. If her career requires eight hours a day, then she really has two full-time jobs—because she's probably going to spend another few hours a day taking care of her family and home. If she needs eight hours' sleep, that doesn't leave a whole lot of time for recreation! She's the one who has to get up a couple of hours early to get the kids off to school, make breakfast for everyone, do the beds, and do whatever else she can before she goes to work. When she comes home, if she's an average career woman, the laundry and vacuuming and cooking and dishwashing will all be waiting for her.

As you can see, it's much more difficult for a woman to have a career than it is for a man. He can be totally committed to his work. He doesn't have to worry about his socks and his food and his house. That job belongs to his wife. He wears just one hat, the *breadwinner hat*.

Of course, a working woman can be every bit as much a breadwinner as her spouse, but she almost always has to wear a lot of other hats, too. She's a wife, mother, chef, laundress, housecleaner, chauffeur, and child psychologist (and sometimes she's a psychologist where her husband is concerned, too). She's also expected to be her husband's errand boy, social director, and lover—she has to find time for everything. What does she need more than anything? I often say she needs a "wife"!

Most husbands today don't seem to resent their wives' working, but they don't want to be neglected either while a woman pursues her career. My Mel was from the old school and he didn't like it when my work interfered with "his" time. He liked to call himself "the chairman of the chairman of the board." When I came home at night, he wanted me to be somebody who was thinking only of him, and I respected that.

It takes me sixteen minutes to drive home from my office every evening, and in that time I would have to take off my chairman-of-the-board hat and replace it with my Mel-Ash's-wife hat. Since Mel liked me to have dinner on as soon as I got home, I planned meals carefully so that was possible. And he liked for me to sit with him for a couple of hours each evening and talk or watch television. I must confess that there were times when I thought, "What a waste of time it is to sit in front of this television set, when I could be getting something done!" But I loved Mel, and I knew he was sensitive and needed that time with me. Perhaps it was the workaholic in me that sometimes made it hard to relax and do nothing.

Once in a while, I tried to watch television with one eye and read the day's accumulation of mail with the other. But Mel felt that I was using "his" time, and he resented that. Finally I changed my schedule. I'd still go to bed when he did, but I'd get up at five each morning so I could start on my dictation. That way I could do my correspondence and paperwork without Mel feeling I was infringing on his time. Then at seven-thirty, when he got up, I'd change hats again and become Mel Ash's wife.

Fortunately, by then I was able to afford a housekeeper to do many of the household tasks I would otherwise have had to do. I no longer wear the hats of a window cleaner, a floor scrubber, or a laundress! But there were times in my life as a working wife and mother when I had no alternative than to do my own housework, because I couldn't afford to hire anyone to fill in for me. With the high cost of living today, I'm sure many working women are in the same boat I was in back then. Even though I have a housekeeper now, I still work as many hours a day as I always did. But now I'm able to wear my executive hat more hours of the day and there are some other hats I rarely have to put on.

A working woman has to be careful that she doesn't try to wear *too* many hats. I think the most exhausting time of my life was when I was raising my three children, working as a Stanley dealer—and I decided to add another hat and become a college student. I had been married ten years, and I had always dreamed of becoming a doctor, and I thought *now* was the time! This was back in the days when it was considered a waste of time for a married woman to go back to school, so I felt I had to conceal being one. Then, college was something you did full time, and they didn't look kindly on women who were also working, so I had to conceal that, too. I dressed the role of a student so I could fit in, down to wearing bobbysocks. I even took off my wedding ring and wore it around my neck.

And I never mentioned to anybody that I had three children at home!

I usually had classes in the morning and a Stanley party in the afternoon. When I got home, I'd clean house, wash diapers, cook meals, and so on. The problem was, I was too tired to study after all that. Sometimes I'd go to bed shortly after the children did, and set my clock for three in the morning. I'd get up at three, drink some coffee to wake myself up, and then study until the children woke up around seven. Finally, I just couldn't keep up the pace. I was about to have a nervous breakdown, because I was burning the candle at both ends. But while I was doing all that, I had discovered that I really enjoyed sales and that I was good at it! I had taken a three-day-long aptitude test when I started college. One day, the dean called me in to discuss the results. She told me that my scores in scientific endeavor, though good, were far surpassed by my scores in other areas—such as persuasion. She highly recommended that I change my courses to marketing and possibly pursue a career as a buyer. She pointed out that in a matter of four years I could probably make excellent money as a professional salesperson or buyer for a large department store (she wasn't aware that I was *already* pursuing a sales career in my spare time that was not only supporting my children but paying my college tuition!).

And she argued that all in all, two years would be required for pre-med, a minimum of four years more in college (probably six or eight), and then internship, which meant that getting into practice was ten or twelve years away. She definitely felt I should opt for the shorter route to a well-paying career.

Once I dropped out of college to sell Stanley full time, I was still working long hours—at both my sales job and my *family* job—but my schedule wasn't quite so hectic. The fact that I was working on a straight commission basis was an advantage. It meant that I could work *my* time, not company time. I don't believe I could ever have been a full-time mother if I'd been required to be at a desk job nine to five every day. I needed the flexibility my sales job offered, so I could be with my children when they needed me. I arranged my Stanley parties so I was home after school to greet my children, prepare their dinner, and give them my full attention.

Many of our Mary Kay Consultants say that the flexibility of their work hours is one of the most important aspects of their job. When you consider all those other hats a working woman wears, she really needs a job she can fit in around her other responsibilities. What does a nine-to-five working mother do when little Johnny has a 103-degree fever and she *has* to be at work that day? For emergencies like that, we have what we call a "dovetail system." If one of our Beauty Consultants is ill or has a family emergency, she just calls another Consultant, who holds the scheduled Beauty Show in her place. This way, a woman can stay home when a child is ill or there's some other emergency.

I think it's the nine-to-five job that really puts pressure on a working woman. My administrative assistant, Jennifer Pruitt, for instance, comes in at eight-thirty in the morning and doesn't leave until five. When her baby was small, she would actually go home at noon every day to spend some time with her. Naturally, that was hard for her to manage, but she did it. And, of course, she has all the other things to do when she gets home at night, like cooking dinner and cleaning house. Jennifer is a terrific assistant to me—but she's also devoted to her family.

I know many women do manage to wear all those hats, but it can certainly take its toll. In order to be effective in their careers and still be good wives and mothers, they must be organized. As a general rule, I have found that getting organized is one of the biggest problems working women have. And if a woman is trying to wear a great many hats and she isn't organized, she's operating under a tremendous handicap.

Of course, some of the menial work women do (like laundry, scrubbing floors, and so on) really could be done by a housekeeper. But with inflation, many women simply can't afford to hire a housekeeper. So that puts the working woman right back to square one. If she *can* afford someone, I think it's a terrific investment. Even if she only has someone one day a week to clean the house thoroughly, it will give her time that she can use more valuably.

I think many women feel guilty about working because they can't spend as much time as they would like with their children. When they get home at night, they're already tired, and then they have housekeeping to do. There simply *isn't* enough time for the children. But if a woman delegates some of those household tasks to a housekeeper, she has more time and energy for the family. This often makes it possible for her to come home after work and devote one or two hours of undivided attention to her children.

I've often said, "It's not the *quantity* of time you spend with your children that counts, it's the *quality* of time." I think a lot of people make the mistake of thinking that just being in the proximity of her children makes a woman a good mother. But in many cases, a woman is not paying any attention to her children at all. In fact, a mother who's with her children all day long sometimes gets the "screaming-meemies" by five o'clock and she's shouting, "Don't ask me that question again!" That's not being a good mother—she just happens to be there. I found that when I was away from my children for a few hours a day, I was a better mother than when I was there all day long. They seemed to appreciate me more and I was more patient with them.

Being a working mother helped me to remember my priorities: God first, family second, career third. I think working women can easily make the mistake of getting caught up in too many outside activities. While community and civic work is very important, I don't think it should be done at the expense of our families. If the P.T.A. is important for your child's sake, I'm all for it. But if it's just a social occasion for you, then perhaps you should eliminate it. A working woman has to decide how much time she has and which activities she can afford to participate in.

It takes a great deal of time and energy for a woman to really care for her family and build her career at the same time. She has to take off some of those other hats if she's to survive—and succeed—and concentrate on her major priorities. My mother used to say, "You can't chase two rabbits and catch either one"—and she was right!

~ 9 ~

The Career Woman and Her Husband

With so many hats to wear, a career woman is likely to be running in several directions at the same time—trying to chase a lot of rabbits and not catching any! But her biggest problem can sometimes be her husband. When a woman devotes time and energy to her career, her husband often feels short-changed. And in my opinion, no amount of success in the world is worth sacrificing a good marriage. Thankfully, a woman who keeps her wits about her doesn't have to choose between her husband and her career. She can have both! But that kind of utopia doesn't just happen automatically. *You have to make it happen.*

Stop and think for a few minutes how your husband might be feeling. Suppose you've always been a full-time wife and mother, and now suddenly you have a career. The truth is, your husband has probably become a bit spoiled over the years. He's used to the luxury of a full-time wife, mother, cook, housekeeper—all those roles we talked about before. Then suddenly, everything changes. You're excited about your new job. But *he's* not getting as much attention as you used to give him. Your career represents competition to him. He may feel threatened. No wonder he resents your job!

Although your husband may not recognize it at first, there are many ways your career will benefit him and the family. In our company, we have found that a woman who might not have taken care of her personal appearance suddenly becomes very conscious of it. She wants to be as well groomed and well dressed as the other Consultants with whom she works. Not only is her face prettier, but she starts to do something about her hair and nails, too. The first thing she'll do in the morning is put on her makeup, and when she's done that she wants to put on a pretty dress. It doesn't take her husband long to notice her new look. We've found that he's usually very pleased with the transformation of his wife.

When a woman is no longer surrounded by the same four walls every day, she becomes a more interesting wife. She knows how to talk about something besides dishes and diapers and debts. Which reminds me of a story about a woman with several small children who spent most of her time at home with them. One night, her husband took her to a formal dinner, and she found herself seated next to a VIP. When a long silence prevailed, she thought, "I've got to say something, I've just got to say something, what will I say?" Finally she turned to him and said, "I'll bet I can eat my spinach before you do!"

But at first, your husband may not recognize the advantages of your career. He's more likely to notice that eight hours of your day which he thought of as "his" time aren't his any more. Suddenly you're not always available to run his errands, and you're obviously not spending as many hours in the kitchen as you formerly did.

I'm often asked how important it is for a woman to have her husband's full support of her career. My answer is, "A woman who has her husband *with her* is a woman and a half. A woman who doesn't have her husband with her is half a woman." (That is certainly not to say that if you don't *have* a husband, you are half a woman!) What I'm saying is that the first sale a married woman needs to make is to "sell" her husband on her new job opportunity. If he resents your career and constantly puts obstacles in your way, it's almost impossible to succeed in a sales job or, for that matter, any other job.

If she doesn't make that sale, she's in for some serious trouble. In our business, for example, it can be disastrous for a woman to have a husband who gets upset when she comes home an hour late from an evening Beauty Show. If she walks in and he says, "For crying out loud, how long did that Show take, anyway? Where have you been?" she's bound to be affected by it. During her next show, she's going to be constantly worried about the time. She will start to cut corners to save time and when she does that, she will be losing sales, and giving up her chance to book future Shows. She will also lose recruits, because the best time to talk with someone about being a Consultant is right after a successful Show. Try as she might, if she's anxious about getting home, she won't be able to do a very good job.

We believe it's essential for our Consultants to have their husbands' support and cooperation, and we do everything we can to help them get it. When a Consultant enters Director Training, we write to thank her husband for his support. We also invite husbands to attend workshops and seminars where the husbands' classes are held. We want each husband to understand what his wife is doing, and how important her work can be to their family life. Our husbands' classes are conducted by other husbands. I believe it was the Packard Motor Car Company that used to have the slogan, "Ask the man who owns one." I guess we're using that philosophy. We feel successful Consultants' and Directors' husbands are best qualified to talk about the advantages of supporting their wives' careers.

At a recent Seminar, every husband in the class received a button that said, "She's Fantastic!" Imagine the reaction that got from people: "Who's fantastic?" He would naturally reply, "My wife!" That gave him a chance to talk about her and her career. Those buttons really built enthusiasm, and they resulted in many husbands finding recruits for their wives. We always give the husbands a little something like that to take home. One year, it was a bumper sticker that read, "Ask Me

About My Wife's Career." We have found that one of the sur-
est ways of getting a husband enthusiastic about his wife's
career is to have him attend Seminar. He almost invariably
leaves feeling that anything those other wives have done, *his*
can do *better!*

If you are a working woman, getting your husband involved is so important! It's always been my observation that
people will support that which they help to create. When a woman
goes to work, she must not only sell her husband on her career, but if she's wise, she'll find ways to get him involved.
Once he's involved, she'll get his support. One area where
many of our Beauty Consultants have gotten their husbands
involved is in the bookkeeping and record keeping that goes
with any business. Many sales-oriented women don't especially like record keeping, so they welcome their husbands' help
in this area, and it's been our experience that most husbands
enjoy keeping their wives' records. Some men who don't like
the bookkeeping end of it help by making reorder deliveries
for their wives. And many men baby-sit in the evening when
their wives are doing Shows. One man wrote recently to
thank me for this involvement, saying that for the first time
he had gotten to *know* his children and to appreciate more
fully what he had formerly thought was his wife's responsibility. Mary Kay Cosmetics has always been family-oriented. I
am most pleased to receive countless letters each day from
Consultants, Directors, and many times from their husbands
and children, telling me of how their family has been brought
together through their involvement with the company. It
makes me especially happy to know of the pride they all seem
to feel in being part of our company.

For example:

Early in my Stanley sales career, I didn't have a husband
to get involved, so I got my children involved instead. I used
to put the money I collected from each hostess into an envelope. On "delivery day," I would come home and pour it all
out in the middle of the living room rug. The children would

sit down and sort and count it. They also helped in filling orders and sometimes in making deliveries. And, just as my children felt involved in helping earn the family income, a husband becomes involved and enthusiastic if a Consultant brings him into her business.

While it's good to have your husband involved in your career, you must be careful not to bring your problems home to him. Sometimes women make the mistake of discussing every little problem at home, and this only serves to upset their husbands. For example, not long ago I received a harsh letter from the husband of one of our Directors. He detailed all the things he believed were wrong with our operation, and just what he thought about every one of the problems. As it turned out, the *real* problem was that his wife had a habit of confiding to him every little tiny thing that upset her. Naturally, he took her side on everything, and the situation blew all out of proportion.

I wrote him and tried to soothe his feelings, and shortly after that I was able to see her at a meeting.

"You're making a mistake I used to make," I told her. "I used to tell Mel all about the little problems that annoyed me at the office. And he would roll them all into a big ball and get mad at everybody who was hurting his dear little wife."

She heard me out and then said, "You know, Mary Kay, you're absolutely right. I *was* bringing home all those little annoyances. And he *was* rolling them up and magnifying them. Things aren't nearly as bad as he made them out to be."

She decided to stop telling him about her petty annoyances and instead began to tell him about a lot of the good things that happened. She recently wrote and told me that everything's all right now. I haven't heard from him again— and her unit production is soaring.

Another mistake we often make as women is to talk too much about our work to our husbands. Even if you're very involved in your career, you have to learn to click it off like a television set. You must remember that he's not as interested in what you're doing as you are. In my case, I tried not to tell Mel about my problems, but I shared little tidbits that I thought he would find interesting.

"Oh, let me tell you about something great that happened today," I'd say. And if I saw he wasn't especially interested in what I was talking about, I'd stop. A woman has to be sensitive to her husband and how he feels and how interested he is. Mel showed me the same consideration. He knew I wasn't interested in every little detail about the stock market, so he didn't go into great detail—except that every time Mary Kay stock made a good move upward, he would excitedly call Richard and me to tell us the good news. He was so proud of our company and of me.

One thing that can really cause tension in a marriage is when a career woman thinks of her earnings as "my money." That's a very serious mistake. Her husband will resent a situation where it's "my money versus your money." But for some reason, many women think that as soon as they go out and earn money, it belongs only to them. I believe in many cases that's because this is a relatively new experience. After all, when her husband brings home his pay check, he deposits it in their joint checking account, and it's *their* money.

A smart woman will also make sure that she spends a certain amount of time with her family—and takes her mind completely off her business. If she doesn't, her husband and children will feel that they're being put aside in favor of her career. She should consciously set aside certain hours of the day and make a habit of spending that time with the family.

Husbands especially need to feel that there's a certain amount of your time that's all theirs. Mel always liked to see me home at seven each evening. In fact, he had a little fixation about it. If I arrived one minute before seven, everything was fine. But if I was one minute late, he would be upset. I'm not sure exactly how this happened, but that's the way it came to be—and I knew he'd always be waiting for me. After five, I found I could get quite a lot accomplished at the office. When almost everyone had left and the telephones had stopped ringing, we could sit down and do some serious thinking. Often we became so involved, we didn't even realize how late it was. But I would watch the clock. I knew it took me sixteen minutes to drive home, and at twenty minutes till seven I would leave, regardless. I did this because I knew how Mel felt, and his feelings were important to me.

Of course, by seven Mel had quite an appetite, and he wanted dinner on the table as soon as possible. I'd usually have the housekeeper set the table and fix a salad and have it waiting in the refrigerator, and I would plan oven meals that she could prepare and put in, so I would only have to take them out and serve them. But once in a while, I'd be stuck for a dinner. When that happened, I'd pop a good-quality frozen dinner on a plate and put it in the microwave. Mel used to brag that I never served him a TV dinner, but I did sometimes—on a plate!

I remember one of our Beauty Consultants telling me what she did when she got home late and didn't have anything cooking for dinner. She'd throw an onion in a pot of boiling water, and it would smell like something good was cooking for dinner. Her husband would come in a few minutes later and that wonderful aroma made him feel a good meal was under way. In the meantime, she'd have time to pull something out of the freezer. While some people might not appreciate what she did, it kept her husband happy—and that's all that really mattered to her.

I think it's important for women to realize how sensitive their husbands can be. Women don't have a monopoly on feelings; men can be just as easily hurt. For instance, they say men can take criticism. I just don't believe it. Criticism must be given tactfully, no matter who you're dealing with. And whatever you do, rule number one is: don't ever put your husband down in public no matter what he does. If he does something you really don't like, then let him know privately how you feel—in a subtle way. But don't make such an issue of it that you hurt his feelings.

I learned how sensitive men can be to criticism when Mel bought himself a vicuña coat. He'd always wanted one, and he was very proud of his purchase. It was quite expensive, and the material was really beautiful. But the buttons just did not match the quality of the coat.

So I admired it, and then I made a mistake. I said, "I don't understand why they would put such cheap buttons on such a beautiful, expensive coat."

I regretted that ever after, because once I'd said that, Mel wouldn't wear the coat. Every so often I'd say, "Why don't you wear your vicuña coat?"

"You don't like it," he'd say.

It wasn't that I didn't like the coat—I just wanted to change the buttons. But he never would let me change the buttons, and he never would wear the coat. And all because of my tactless remark. As I said, I don't think men can take criticism any better than women. A wife has to be very careful in what she says to her husband—and not just to him, but to *everyone.*

It's important to realize that every person has an ego, and some people need to be handled very delicately. Now, Mel had retired, so perhaps my career presented more of a threat to him than if he had been actively involved in his own career. He did spend a large portion of his day at Merrill Lynch, where he avidly followed the stock market. But, especially during an economic slump, how exciting can the market be? It had to be very difficult to be married to me, because whenever we went out socially, people always ended up talking about Mary Kay Cosmetics after a few brief remarks to Mel about market conditions. That kind of thing can be very damaging to a man's ego, especially a man like Mel.

Although Mel was retired and I had money coming in from the company and from investments, he always insisted on paying all the bills for the house. He felt it was his prerogative to pay the gas, electric, and water bills, as well as bills for any maintenance that was needed. He wouldn't even let me see the bills. For my part, I paid for a lot of little things, but I had to be sure he wasn't aware of them.

I never knew whether or not Mel knew of some of these little things. But caring for your spouse is a two-way street, and Mel did something very thoughtful for me that I had never heard of another husband doing—his Thursday gifts. We were married on a Thursday, so from the beginning, Thursday became a special day to us. And every Thursday for the fourteen years we were married, Mel brought me a gift. Depending on his mood and his financial situation, the gifts ranged from a flower to a piece of peanut brittle to a diamond. But no matter what, every single Thursday when I came home, he'd have a gift-wrapped package with a card waiting for me in my dressing room. He was really so thoughtful and caring. He was generous with compliments, too. He told me how beautiful I looked every morning and you know that wasn't true. I went to bed Elizabeth Taylor and woke up Charles de Gaulle on a daily basis! Because I wanted to "live up" to that image, I was out of bed before Mel was awake every morning trying to look "beautiful" for him. I wanted to put my makeup on before he put his spectacles on! Many times he would call just to say, "I love you." It was wonderful.

Because Mel was from the old school, he felt that certain responsibilities were the man's, and that was the way it had to be. However, this doesn't have to be the same in every household. Sue Kirkpatrick, one of our outstanding Directors, has a very different arrangement with her husband, Kirk.

Sue was not serious about her Mary Kay career until a few years ago, when Kirk lost his job as manager of a radio station in New Castle, Indiana. Well, New Castle is a town of 20,000, and there wasn't much Kirk could do there except wait it out. They didn't want to sell their home and upset their lives by moving to another community.

They sat down and talked about it, and they realized that Sue's Mary Kay career was the only job they had between the two of them. So they made a decision that *he* would stay home and care for the house and children, and she would work for Mary Kay on a full-time basis. And she was fantastic! She ended up second in the nation in sales in both 1979 and 1980. She never could have done it without Kirk's support.

Sue enjoys joking about their role reversal. She says that one day she came home and he was busy vacuuming, wearing an apron, and perspiration was pouring down his face. She looked at him and said, "You know, the least you could do when I come home is look nice!" How's that for putting the shoe on the other foot?

Sue is very fortunate to have such a supportive husband. Kirk conducted a class at Seminar last year, and told about how his wife took over when things got bad. It had quite an impact on everyone. And Kirk has no problem with Sue being the breadwinner. It's like one of the other husbands said, when somebody asked him how it felt to have his wife making more money than he did. He answered, "As long as we're playing a tune, I don't care who's got the fiddle."

At Mary Kay, we have quite a few women who are earning more money than their husbands. We know that can create a problem for a man. Naturally, if a woman isn't used to it, she needs help in handling it. Briefly, the best advice I can give is, "Spend it on things that are needed, but don't rub it in." A woman can go out and buy a new carpet for the living room, and her husband probably will never know what it costs—as long as she doesn't tell him.

It's most fulfilling to build a successful career, but if you lose your husband and family in the process, then I think you have failed. Success is so much more wonderful when you have someone to share it with. It's no fun to come home and count your money by yourself.

⮌10⮍
The $35,000 List

When I was just beginning my sales career, I had the good fortune to hear a motivational speaker tell a story that made a lasting impression on me. His subject was time management, and the story concerned Ivy Lee, the leading efficiency expert of his day, and Charles Schwab, who was the president of Bethlehem Steel, which was just a small company at the time.

Ivy Lee called on Mr. Schwab and said to him, "I can increase your efficiency—and your sales—if you will allow me to spend fifteen minutes with each of your executives."

Naturally, Mr. Schwab asked him, "What will it cost me?"

"Nothing," Mr. Lee said, "unless it works. In three months, you can send me a check for whatever you think it's worth to you. Fair enough?"

Mr. Schwab thought it was. So Ivy Lee spent fifteen minutes with each of the executives. The only thing he did was to exact a promise from each man. For the next three months, before he left his desk at the end of the day, he would make a list of the six most important things he had to do the next day, and number them in order of their importance.

"Each morning, begin with the first item on your list," he told them, "and scratch it off when it's finished. Just work your way right down the list. If you don't get something done, it goes on the next day's list."

At the end of the three-month period, efficiency and sales had increased to such an extent that Mr. Schwab sent Ivy Lee a check for $35,000!

I was very impressed with this story. I thought that if that list was worth $35,000 to Charles Schwab, it was worth thirty-five cents to me. So that very day, sitting there in the audience, I got out an old envelope and started writing down the six most important things I had to do the next day. It worked so well that I've made up a $35,000 list every day of my life ever since.

Somehow, you get so much more done this way than if you just go helter-skelter in any old direction. My list of the six most important things keeps me from getting off track. And it's so easy for a woman to get off track, because there are just so many things we have to get done. I can walk into any room in my house and see six things that need to be done today—at least, that's what I think. But actually, do they? Are they *the most important things* I could be doing? Or can they wait while something *more important* gets done?

Sometimes when you're tired in the evening, it's tempting to just run over tomorrow's list in your head, but I've found it's essential to write it down. Once it's on paper, it gets programmed into your subconscious. Often I find I'm so busy I don't even have time to refer to it during the day. But by the time I do take a look at the list, I've already done most of the things on it, because subconsciously I remembered what I had written down.

Just the same, it's essential to have the list on your bedside table, or in the kitchen, or at your desk, wherever you'll see it first thing in the morning. Then you have to *adhere* to it. Don't let yourself be sidetracked by extraneous things. So often you'll notice something like, "Oh my, those curtains have got to come down." Maybe they do—but not today! A career woman has so many distractions, with all the hats she wears, that all sorts of things are bound to pop up. But you cannot allow yourself to get off track. If you must do such things, put them on the list for the next day.

It's also important to limit your list to *just six* items. Don't be overzealous and put down seventeen. If you do, you'll start to think, "I can't possibly do all this." You'll be so over-whelmed that you'll end up not getting anything done. If you can accomplish those six things, you've accomplished a lot. Once you get those six things done, you have my blessings— take the rest of the day off.

I really believe in lists. In fact, I even make a list for my housekeeper of things she might miss. She does a marvelous job, but every now and then I'll notice a spot on the dining room rug, or I'll realize that the runners on the sliding doors need to be cleaned. These are things she may overlook if I don't write them down for her.

To many women, a housekeeper sounds like an extrava-gance. I remember saying for the first ten years of my career, "As soon as I can afford a housekeeper, I'm going to have one." Well, if you've been saying that too, let me give you this advice: *you can't afford not to have a housekeeper.* Hiring a housekeeper is the best thing a career woman can do to free up her time. You must always remember that your time is the most important thing you have—and you've got to make it count. There are people where you live who will be happy to become your housekeeper. They *need* the job!

Do you realize that the president of the United States has the same amount of time you have? But look what he gets done! By ten in the morning, he's cut a ribbon on a dam, signed seven bills into law, and had a press conference. And most people are still on their second cup of coffee! He has to know how to make his time count. Each of us has just twenty-four hours every day. It's what you *do* with your twenty-four hours that makes the difference.

Now, the way to use your twenty-four hours is not scrub-bing floors and washing dirty dishes and ironing clothes all day. I often tell our Beauty Consultants that they can make more than enough money in one productive hour on the telephone to pay for the services of a housekeeper for the whole day. So what sense does it make to be doing those tasks when you can hire someone else to do them? It doesn't matter who does those things—as long as you don't! Don't worry about "ironing love" into your husband's collar; he doesn't know about it and he doesn't care. He just wants a clean shirt when he reaches for it. *Get someone else to do it.*

It might take a while before you can find a housekeeper to do things the way you like them done. Why, I'm so particular that I have to have the towels folded a certain way before they're put in the kitchen drawer. If someone folds them another way, I want them refolded. But I taught my housekeeper how to do it for me, and you can teach somebody how to do it for you. Okay, it might take a month to train somebody. So take a month, and train somebody!

The important thing to remember is to *get somebody else to do the things that aren't important for you to do personally.* One of the best things I ever did was make a list of all the tasks I spent my time on every day. Then I checked off the ones that nobody could do for me. These were the things I had to do, and I concentrated on them. I had someone else to do all the rest. You are the only one who knows what really matters to you. If you think it's important for your child that you attend a P.T.A. meeting, then by all means, do it. Whatever is really important to you and your family is what you should be doing.

I had heard "hire a housekeeper" for ten years after I went to work as a salesperson. I saw other women succeeding while I was not because they were free to use their time more productively. Well, I still thought I couldn't afford a housekeeper, but on sheer faith I put an ad in the newspaper one weekend. Then I waited for a response. Every time I started to think about paying a housekeeper, my heart would pound, because I really couldn't even afford to pay for the ad!

"My loving mother"

Baby Mary Kay

At the age of seven

High-school graduation

As a young saleswoman

Mary Kay's office staff and building, 1964

The international headquarters of Mary Kay Cosmetics, Dallas

Mary Kay in 1973

With husband Mel Ash, 1979

With her family

I needed someone who could do *everything,* so I had put all the requirements in the ad: cooking, cleaning, caring for three children, and so on. I ended the ad by stating the salary I was able to pay. I thought, "Anybody who's crazy enough to answer this ad is really asking for it!"

But on Sunday afternoon, a woman did apply. Mabel was a beautiful person, well dressed and quite lovely. I'll never forget how thrilled I was when she accepted the position. I thought, "How can I be so lucky?" Then I began worrying about how I would pay her. She would be starting on Monday morning.

Talk about being motivated! I had never booked so many parties, sold so much, or recruited as many people as I did that week—because I had to have enough extra for Mabel's salary by the end of the week! I was out of that house at eight in the morning booking, selling, and recruiting. I worked harder than I ever had before. But the end result was that I made enough money to pay both of us, because she relieved me of so much of my housework. I found that my first Monday morning goal was to earn enough to pay her salary on Friday. Then the rest of the week, whatever I earned was mine. It worked out so well that Mabel stayed with me for nine years.

Having a housekeeper has been so great for me that ever since I've been encouraging other career women to hire housekeepers. If you're still scrubbing floors, you've got to stop it! As one of our Directors once said, "I've been scrubbing the same spot in my house all my life—and it's still dirty." And it's going to be dirty. So get someone else to do that. Delegate your work. *Stop spending dollar time on penny jobs.* And do the things that are important to your family. If it's important to you to spend three hours sometime during the day with your children (and it should be), then find a way to do it. If the only way to do this is to hire somebody else to cook dinner, then you know what you have to do!

Whether or not you have a housekeeper, it's still important to be organized. Let me give you a tip that I think helps any woman keep house a little more easily. Instead of trying to clean the whole house at one given time, I instruct my housekeeper to clean *one room thoroughly* every day. Now, I mean really go over it from top to bottom. I'm talking about going up around the ceiling, getting the cobwebs, dusting, vacuuming, polishing the furniture, everything. If this is done one room at a time, by the end of the week the entire house will have been cleaned. I do the same thing with cleaning out drawers. I love well-organized drawers, so I'll take one week to clean out all the drawers in a room. I just straighten one every morning, very quickly, and at the end of the week, all the drawers are in order.

Getting your grocery shopping organized can also save lots and lots of time. Most women have a tendency to shop too often. Some of them just stop by the store every night after work. But shopping once a week saves time and money. First of all, you save the gasoline used by going back and forth to the market. Second, there's no way in the world you can just run into the store and get a loaf of bread and some milk. I always say the smartest salesperson who ever lived is the fellow who invented the shopping cart. Somehow, when you run in for just one item you end up spending $22.80 in five minutes. So shop once a week, and when you go, take a list. And stick to the list. Oh, and incidentally, don't shop when you are hungry!

I have a plastic memo board in my kitchen with a kind of chalk you can erase with a damp cloth. Anytime I use up the last of anything, I put the item on the memo board then and there, so I don't forget. Then, before I go to the grocery store, I put my list on a piece of paper, and I make sure I stick to it. I have to confess that I also collect coupons for my groceries—I think the clerks at the local supermarket get a "charge" out of that! But I keep a little clip-it knife in a box on my coffee table, so when I read the paper or a magazine and find a coupon for a product I use, it's handy. I put the coupons in an alphabetical file, the kind they sell to keep your checks in. So coffee is filed under *C*, vegetables under *V*, and so on. When I'm ready to shop, I just thumb through the right section for whatever coupons I need for the items on my list, noting the brand. It takes very little time, and I feel good about that two or three dollars the clerk returns to me when she finishes checking my groceries! It's fun!

Along the same line, in my house we wash clothes only once a week, not every day. And I never wash unless I have a full load. This saves energy, and it also saves time, because it takes just about as long to put a half load of clothes in the washer and dryer as a full load. I don't run the dishwasher either until it's full.

Even a woman with a housekeeper often ends up doing a great deal of cooking. I like a nice breakfast, and for years I have used a time-saving biscuit mix for breakfast time. Instead of mixing biscuits every morning, and going through all the measuring and cutting in the shortening, I make a big batch of biscuit mix, except that I don't stir in the milk. I store it on a shelf in an ice bucket with a tight-fitting lid. In the morning, I take one heaping tablespoon of that mix for each biscuit I want, add a little milk, and roll them out. Since there are just a few, I bake them in a little counter-top toaster-broiler I have, and the bacon and eggs are done by the time they're ready. The same mix works for pancakes. You just add more milk and a little sugar.

With all the hats we wear, working women have to be creative about organizing our meals. We have a top Consultant on the island of Guam who's a shining example of organization. She has *ten children*—and a husband who likes the whole family to sit down to a hot meal at noon every day. She was holding two Shows every day and was Queen of Sales in her unit and still managing that. When I met her, I asked her, "How in the world are you doing it?"

She told me her method. She didn't hold any Shows on Saturdays. Instead, she spent the day at home with the family, and on that one day she cooked enough meals for the next week and froze them. Then each weekday morning, the children helped her set the table and get breakfast on, and after breakfast they helped clear the table and set it up for the noon meal, the big meal of the day in Guam. She'd take out one of those frozen meals, set her automatic oven timer, make a salad, and off she'd go to her 9:00 A.M. Show. At eleven-thirty, when she got home, the meal was cooking away. And by twelve, when her husband came home, that homemade hot meal was on the table. After lunch, she was off to her one-thirty Show and got home by four to greet her children home from school. *That's* being organized!

That Consultant saved a lot of time by delegating work around the house, and I believe every woman should do that. In addition to helping me fill orders, my children all had household responsibilities. I really believe children should have duties, regardless of a family's financial circumstances. They had to care for their own rooms and do various other things, like gardening, raking leaves, washing dishes, and taking out the garbage. I used to put a chart on the wall listing their daily duties. Each day, I rated their work, and I put up little stars for good performance. I used gold, silver, and red stars, depending on how well they had done their jobs. A child with gold stars would get the maximum allowance for that week. So even when they were little, my children were paid on a work-performance basis, and I believe it taught them the consequences of not doing a good job.

In organizing my housework, I always keep in mind Parkinson's law: "Work expands to fill the time available for it." To prove how true that is, just think back on a time when perhaps an out-of-town friend called to say, "Hi, we're on the outskirts of town and we'll be there in thirty minutes!" You might not have been expecting them, but somehow you managed to get your spring housecleaning done in half an hour. If you had had all day to do the same work, it would have taken all day! The same thing is true if your husband comes home and says, "Guess what? I just won a trip to Acapulco. We're leaving in the morning." You manage to do in one evening what would normally take you two weeks.

Parkinson's law really is true, and I try to bear it in mind. What I do is give myself time limits. When I did my own laundry, I'd allow myself three minutes to iron a shirt. If I was making beds, I'd allot two minutes to a bed. Or I'd see if I could clean the kitchen in ten minutes. I made a game out of it—Beat the Clock! This was good for me, because it reminded me that my time was valuable, no matter what I was doing. *Time is just too precious to be wasted.*

I have my work organized, too. For instance, I don't like working on a cluttered desk. I like to have everything in its place before I leave at night, and then the following day I start work with a clean desk. I have it arranged so that the work I haven't done is put in a red folder, and that comes home with me every night. If there's anything that doesn't have to have action taken on it but that I do want to read, it goes in my To Read file.

When I arrive at the office in the morning, my secretary has arranged everything that's on the desk. Now, instead of shuffling through everything and picking out the "goodies," which we are all prone to do, I start with whatever's on top— no matter what it is. Even if it takes me two hours of research to get the answers to the questions in that top letter, I don't go on until I've finished with it. I go through everything in order, and that's how I work my way down to the bottom of the pile. I handle every piece of paper only *one* time—I think that's very important. Otherwise, you pick up a letter and say, "Gee, I don't know how to answer that, I'll have to think about it for a while." Then you put it aside, and you pick it up a couple of hours later, and you still don't do anything. It's better to make a decision. The more you shuffle a piece of paper without making a decision, the more time you waste. It's only human to want to procrastinate when it comes to difficult decisions. But it's really very poor time management.

As you can see, I really believe in getting on with the

work at hand. It seems to me that a great many people spend more time worrying about something than it would take them to go ahead and do it. They worry their way through a whole day, with nothing accomplished. Often it's because they don't want to make a decision. But in most cases, the first decision you come to is the right one. You must have confidence in yourself, and go ahead and make a decision. Otherwise, you lose time and energy worrying about it!

I try to save time any way I can. One way I do that is by keeping tape recorders in my dressing room and bathroom and car. This way I can listen to motivational tapes while I'm getting dressed and putting on my makeup, and while I'm driving to work. Otherwise, this time would be "down time." I also receive a fair amount of correspondence by tape. I enjoy these tape letters, but many people get a little carried away on tape and go on at some length. So I'll listen to these while I'm dressing, and I keep a pad near my tape recorder to jot down my thoughts while I'm listening. If I'm driving, I often make a note at a traffic light. It saves time for me, and I accomplish something when I would normally have "lost" that time.

Another way I save time during the working day is by eating lunch in my office. I'm often invited to lunch by business associates, but I don't accept the invitations. These "working lunches" can last until two or three in the afternoon. And then normally you eat more than you should and by the time you get back to the office, you don't feel like working at all. The day is just lost! So I prefer a quick, light lunch at my desk.

I've always been time-conscious. There are only twenty-four hours in a day, and all my working life I've tried to get the most mileage out of those hours. Some years ago, I heard someone say that "three early risings make an extra day." I thought about that, and said to myself, "If I get up at five for three mornings, I'll have an eight-day week. That's what I've been looking for!"

I then realized I could take that further. If I got up early *six* times a week, I'd have a nine-day week! I also discovered how much more I could get done during those early morning hours, when there were no phone calls or other interruptions. I found I really liked having that nine-day week. When I talked to other people about it, I'd ask them to join my "Five O'Clock Club."

It's just amazing how many of our Mary Kay people have joined the Five O'Clock Club. Of course, there are some people who are truly night people, and they just cannot function that early in the morning. But I always suggest to our new Directors that they at least try it, and so many of them have written to tell me, "I've just joined the Five O'Clock Club, and I love it! I get so much done before my family even gets up." Helen McVoy, our top National Sales Director, belongs to the club, and she often calls me at six in the morning. She doesn't bother to ask, "Are you up?" She knows I am.

In my speeches, I have often talked about the $35,000 List and the Five O'Clock Club. Then, if my audience is a class of prospective Directors, I'll ask how many want to join the Five O'Clock Club, and I'll get a big show of hands.

I'll say, "Okay, that's great! What I'll do is, one of these mornings I'm going to call you at 5:30 A.M. and I'm going to ask you to read me the six things on your list. Now, how many *still* want to join the Five O'Clock Club?" Surprisingly enough, they still raise their hands. (And I *have* been known to call!)

When you try getting up early to put that extra day in your week, it's sometimes hard to get yourself started. So I always suggest that when a woman gets up, she should fix herself up so she looks presentable before she starts doing her work. This is *so* important to women who work from their homes, and don't go to an office. Getting dressed and putting on makeup lifts a woman's morale, and puts her in a business-like mood. It's too easy for a woman to get in the habit of greeting her family at breakfast in a housecoat, with her hair uncombed—why, she wouldn't even let the garbage man see her like that! A woman who looks good feels better. And getting dressed and putting on makeup gets you ready for work.

Once you're dressed, the first thing to do is start on your list of today's six most important things. Begin with number one—and *don't procrastinate.* Everyone tends to procrastinate on certain things—and these are usually the important things. For instance, we have found that some of our Consultants put off calling their pink tickets. Pink tickets are the Consultant's carbon copies of the customer orders.

Two weeks after a sale, the Consultant is supposed to call the customer to make sure she's happy with her purchase. She asks such questions as, "Are you using your Mary Kay Skin Care?" "Are you getting great results?" "Do you have any questions?" This is strictly a service call, and it lets the customer know we care about her. Let's face it, the companies that sell cosmetics over the counter in department stores don't call their customers. And the call gives the Consultant a chance to find out if the customer is happy with her cosmetics. In some cases, a customer has to be reprogrammed or instructed again on how to use a product. On rare occasions, a Consultant may need to pick up an item and exchange it for another formula or, even more rarely, refund the customer's money. Whatever the case, we're far better off *knowing* a customer is unhappy and doing something about it at once.

So calling pink tickets is really important, and it should be right at the top of a Consultant's list of important things to do. But this happens to be one of those things Consultants tend to procrastinate about because they're afraid of rejection. They fear that someone will say, "Look, I don't have time to talk to you." Or worse, "I don't like your products." This fear isn't in fact realistic. I find that a Consultant who makes two or three pink ticket calls and gets positive, enthusiastic feedback from customers can't wait to get her finger back in that dial! So often it's true that we procrastinate about something because of fear of rejection, when the "death of fear is in doing what you fear to do!"

I constantly tell our Consultants and Directors, "In this

business, you are the only boss you have. I want you to be the most demanding boss you ever had. If you really want to make a success of this business, then you must put yourself on a schedule, so that by eight-thirty in the morning you have your house done—and you must do whatever it takes to get it done. Then you must work from eight-thirty to five and only allow yourself a thirty-minute lunch break, and perhaps a ten-minute coffee break morning and afternoon (that is, if you're working at home) so you can break up your day. If you've done that, then at five, you're off!" We have found that if a Consultant will spend as much time on her Mary Kay work as she would if she were working in an office, she can make twice as much money as she could at any other job and more! And we have Consultants and Directors who are proving this to be true every single day.

If I were to name one quality necessary for success in sales, it would have to be good time management. How a salesperson manages her time will make or break her. A good example is one of our top Consultants, who works in a rural southwestern town with a population of 7,500. Now, you wouldn't expect people in a farming community to be that excited about cosmetics, would you? But this woman is very, very successful.

We asked her how she did it, and she said that she actually books Shows within a 150-mile radius of that little town. But she practices excellent time management. When she sets up a Beauty Show one hundred miles away, she always insists that the hostess book another show for her the same day. That way she doesn't waste her time and money driving so far for a single Show. The difference between this woman and less successful salespeople is good time mangement.

You see, ordinary people with good time management get great results. On the other hand, people who seem to have everything going for them will fail if they fail to manage their time. Often they think they're working when in reality they're just worrying. Worrying about those letters they should have written. Worrying about those phone calls they should have made. And they worry their way through a whole day. My advice has always been, "If you're going to waste a day, just waste the living daylights out of it. But if you're going to work, *work*." One intense hour is worth a dreamy day!

⮑ 11 ⮐
Plan Your Life
Like Your Vacation

Have you ever had one of those Saturdays when you got up in the morning and didn't have a single thing planned for the day? You drift from one thing to another, and by the end of the day you realize you haven't accomplished a thing. You feel empty and depressed and frustrated; you've wasted a day you'll never get a chance to relive. Well, just as you drifted through an entire day, some people drift through a week, a month, a year—and even a lifetime.

But those same people may do a great job planning their vacations! Suppose your husband comes home from work one day and announces, "Honey, I have two weeks' vacation starting September first." All of a sudden you have lots of plans.

"Oh, wonderful! Let's see, where shall we go? How are we going to get there? Where shall we stay? What kind of clothes will the children need?"

Every single detail is worked out. You plan that vacation down to the last item. On September first, you drive out of the driveway for the airport, and you know exactly what you are going to do. As a result, you have a successful trip.

But what happens when you get home? You get back in the same old routine. You get up in the morning, hurry off to the same old job, come home in the evening with nothing planned, watch television, and go to bed. The next day follows the same pattern. At the end of the week, nothing's changed, and you're right back where you were on Monday. And at the end of the month, and the end of the year, you're just where you were a year ago. Without goals, you can waste your whole life, with nothing to show for it but a feeling of frustration and dissatisfaction.

If you were going to drive to your vacation destination, you wouldn't start without a road map. You have to have a road map if you expect to get to your destination. The same thing is true of your life. Without a plan, a road map, you will never get where you want to go. To accomplish anything, you must sit down and decide what you want from life—your long-term goals. It helps to visualize them when you get them on paper.

Sometimes when people do that, their goals seem overwhelming, but, as the old Chinese proverb goes, "The longest journey begins with but a single step." In other words, to accomplish great things, you must achieve one small goal at a time. New Consultants who join Mary Kay are urged to hold five Shows during their first week in business. *It's important to set realistic short-term goals—goals you can actually attain*, and go on to bigger ones as you gain confidence in your ability.

At the same time, a good goal is like a good exercise—it makes you stretch a little. Goals should be slightly out of reach, because if you don't have to stretch for them, you're never going to get very far. When I say, "Shoot for the moon," I don't mean to set ridiculous goals. Set possible goals—but stretch yourself. Because if you shoot for the moon and miss it, you will still be among the beautiful stars.

At a recent Jamboree, I talked to a Beauty Consultant who was just *so* enthusiastic and *so* excited that she had decided to go home and shoot for the moon—she wanted to start producing $1,000 a week in retail sales as soon as she got home. The only problem was that, at the moment, she was producing an average of $400 a week. I suggested to her a smaller, more realistic goal—$500 for the next week. I reminded her of another old quote: "Inch by inch it's a cinch, but by the yard, it's hard." You don't just look at the $500 figure—you break it down into *daily* goals. Now, $500 a week represents a daily goal of $100 each weekday. You book a Show for every day, and if you don't reach the $100 goal at the Show, you come home and begin calling pink tickets. It's really important to set those attainable daily goals—*and meet them.* If you fall behind your goal by $20 one day and $40 another day, by the end of the week you'll be so far behind you will probably just give up.

Remember, you can eat an elephant one bite at a time. In other words, break your goals down into small segments. It really can be fatal to set an enormous goal and try to achieve it all at once. For example, a very ambitious young woman approached me recently for advice. She had some retail experience, and it was her dream to open a national chain of dress shops. She knew all the big cities she wanted to locate in, and she talked about expanding into Canada. But not once did she mention how she was going to operate her *first* store. Finally I said, "Why don't you concentrate on doing a bang-up job on just *one* dress shop in your hometown? Really learn how to operate a single store. *Then,* when you've achieved that, you can plan to open a second one. In the meantime, by trial and error, you will have ironed out all the problems.

"After you have several stores operating successfully in your own city," I continued, "you can expand to another city. Later, you can move into a neighboring state. If you do this, one step at a time, you will eventually be operating a national chain of dress shops." I told her to set her sights on short-term, attainable goals. Otherwise, that great big lifetime dream would be overwhelming. It's great to think big—but be careful to break your big goal into small goals that you *can* achieve by stretching yourself.

You see, the world is full of people who do a lot of dreaming, and have ambitious long-term goals—but who never take that first step. Often it's because they fail to break their big goal into realistic goals. And sometimes there's another reason: the fear of failure. So many people are afraid of failure, and it's certain that if they never try anything, they'll never fail! That's true, but they'll never achieve, either. You have to overcome your fear of defeat and go ahead and get started. Yes, you're going to make mistakes along the way, but you'll be learning, too. You will soon know a lot of things *not* to do! Remember: the death of fear is in doing what you fear to do!

As I have said, *we fail forward to success.* You *will* make mistakes, and sometimes you'll be frustrated in trying to meet your goals. But for every failure, there's an alternative. There *is* an alternate route to success—you just have to find it. When you come to a roadblock, take a detour. Go in another direction. Don't let a stumbling block stop you. Go over, under, around, or through it, but don't give up. Have confidence in yourself, and you'll find another route. Remember, obstacles either "polish us up" *or* "wear us down." A diamond was once just a hunk of coal until it was put under pressure, then polished to perfection.

In the last chapter, I talked about how important it is to put your daily plan down on paper; that $35,000 list of your six most important things to do. I believe it's important to commit your goals to writing. In fact, not only do I advocate putting your goals down in black and white, but in my own case, I used to write my weekly goals on the bathroom mirror with soap! Each week, I set my goals and then I put them right there in front of me for the whole family to view. If my goal was to hold ten Shows during the week, I put it on the mirror. Then, as I held each Show, I made a hash mark to show where I stood. Having that reminder up there really crystallized my thoughts. I found that if I lost a booking, I'd make every attempt to get a new one for that week, because I *expected* myself to hold ten Shows. I did the same thing with other goals. If I wanted to recruit two new people the next week, I wrote it on the mirror.

I found I looked at that list on the bathroom mirror quite

a lot. But I also wrote those goals on paper and attached them to the sun visor of my car, and on my refrigerator, and on my desk. I kept them everywhere, to keep me thinking about what I wanted to do this week. Pretty soon, those goals would be so deeply embedded in my subconscious mind that everything I did was geared to help me reach them. I just automatically did the right things, because I had programmed myself to succeed!

I've had people tell me they wouldn't think of broadcasting their goals like that—what if they fail? But I believe it helps to let other people know what you intend to do. To illustrate that, let me tell you about an experience I had when I first began my career in sales.

I had been with Stanley Home Products for three weeks, and I wanted to attend the company's annual convention in Dallas. At this point, I was averaging about $7 a party, so I knew I had a lot to learn, and I thought that would be a good place to learn. The cost of the trip was $12, including the round trip on a chartered train from Houston to Dallas and three nights in a hotel (so you know how long ago that was!). Well, I didn't have $12, so I had to try to borrow it. At first, I couldn't get anyone to lend me the money. Finally, a friend agreed to do it, but along with the money she gave me a sermon about how I *should* be spending it on shoes for the children, not running off to some "wicked convention like men go to."

I had only one other dress and no suitcase, so I emptied my Stanley case and used that. I didn't know whether or not the $12 included food, so I packed a pound of cheese and a box of crackers just in case! (To this day, I always have cheese and crackers in my room!) I had no extra money at all. So all the bellman got for carrying my suitcase to the room was a very sweet "Thank you." As you can imagine, that didn't go over any better then than it would now!

But the trip was worth it, because those three days changed my life. I watched them crown the top salesperson

Queen of Sales, and with every fiber of my being *I wanted to be where she was.* I sat in the back row of seats in the room, because that's where I belonged. I was so far down the ladder. I had only been with the company three weeks, and my $7 party average was about as low as you could get. The Queen and I were opposite in every way. She was tall, thin, brunette—and successful. I was neither tall nor thin, and I was probably the most unsuccessful person in the room. But I was so impressed with that Queen's crown and the alligator bag they presented to her that I decided on the spot that next year *I would be Queen!*

Among the things they told us that day was, "Hitch your wagon to a star." I hitched to that girl so hard she must have felt it, even from the back row! A second thing they said was, "Get a railroad track to run on." Stanley didn't have a sales manual or written guide to follow at that time. I needed a railroad track. So I went up to the Queen of Sales and begged her to put on a Stanley party some night in her room while we were there. She agreed, probably because my admiration was so obvious. At that party, I took nineteen pages of notes, which I still have to this day! That became my railroad track, and those notes became my springboard to success.

A third thing I learned was, "Tell somebody what you are going to do." I could see immediately that this was very important in setting personal goals—you don't keep them a secret. You broadcast your ambitions. So I thought, "Who do I tell?" I decided that if I was going to tell someone it might as well be the *president* of the company! Can you imagine? There were a thousand people at that convention, and little Mary Kay wearing a hat so awful they laughed about it for ten years. (The worst thing was, I didn't *know* they were laughing about it for nine years). But I marched up to the president, Mr. Frank Stanley Beveridge, and said, "Next year *I* am going to be the Queen."

He should have laughed—I must have looked so ridiculous. And if he'd known he was talking to the newest salesperson, he probably *would* have laughed. But instead, he took my hand and held it for a moment, looked me squarely in the eye, and said, "You know, somehow I think you will." Those few words literally changed my life.

He probably forgot the incident within five minutes. But his words were inscribed in my memory. I had broadcast my goal, and *he* thought I could do it! I couldn't let him down.

All that year, I failed forward to success. I took my nineteen pages of notes from that party and memorized them. Although our personalities were very different, I could see that the words the Queen of Sales used were better than mine. Obviously, she was succeeding and I was failing; I was certainly doing something wrong. So I used *her words,* and immediately my sales jumped from $7 a party to $28. Her presentation became my railroad track until I could work out my own.

At the end of the year, I really *was* Queen of Sales! You will remember that the previous year they had given the Queen an alligator bag and I had set my heart on that prize. An alligator bag at that point was as far out of my reach as anything could be. I even carried a picture of an alligator bag around all year. And wouldn't you know, they changed the prize and gave me something else. I don't even remember what it was—I just know it *wasn't* the alligator bag!

But I became Queen of Sales by setting a goal and then breaking it down into monthly, weekly, and even daily sales goals and then broadcasting it.

At Mary Kay Cosmetics, we've always believed in spelling out just what one has to do to move up the ladder of success. This makes it easy for our Consultants to set their own personal goals. One of the things that had always bothered me about other companies was that nobody let you know what you had to do in order to advance in your job. You just had to work and wait until finally someone said, "Hey, you're a manager!" Well, I decided that if a woman *knew* what she had to do to be successful, she would do it. *She would have direction.*

Our plan in Mary Kay Cosmetics was that everyone would begin as a Consultant. Nobody can buy a position as a Director because my feeling is that you cannot teach somebody to do something you're not an expert at yourself. Back in our company's infancy, two men offered us $100,000 for the exclusive rights to sell our products in a state. We needed that money at the time, but we resisted the temptation, because they didn't know anything about our business and we didn't want to be in the franchise business. I told one of the men he could have the whole United States territory for only $50—the cost of a show case at that time—but added that the only way he could really succeed was by holding lots of Shows. He hung up!

Once a Consultant learns how to sell our products and recruits three new people, she becomes a Star Recruiter. When she has five people, she becomes a Team Leader. When she has eight people, she's a Future Director. She understands that it's her responsibility to teach her new recruits everything she knows—in order to help them succeed.

A Consultant who has twelve recruits who are doing well may put in her *letter of intent*, stating that she would like to become a Director. The Director of her unit must recommend her, and her letter of intent must meet the requirements. If we feel she's Director material, we invite her to Dallas to become a DIQ, Director in Qualification.

Every step of the way, our Consultants and Directors *know* what they have to do to climb the ladder of success, so they can set clear, attainable goals for themselves. A Consultant who comes to Dallas for her DIQ week (held one week a month) knows she will pay all her own expenses for transportation and hotel; we provide meals. She will also work very hard during that week, because the training sessions sometimes last from seven in the morning until late in the evening. She goes home with full knowledge of exactly what she needs to do to fulfill her goal of becoming a Director.

During the next three-month period, a DIQ has specific

sales goals to maintain, on an escalated scale. And at the end of that period, she must not only have achieved monthly sales quotas, she must also increase her unit size to a minimum of twenty-four Consultants. At the end of three months, if she has met the requirements, she becomes a Sales Director and is eligible to receive the commission on the people she has recruited and trained.

We set twenty-four recruits as a realistic minimum, but our DIQs are constantly reminded, "You don't want to be a minimum person; so we suggest you shoot for the moon and try to have forty or fifty Consultants instead of twenty-four." We know that spelling out what we expect from our people gives them direction. It helps to establish clear-cut goals.

A woman who becomes a Director has already achieved a great deal—but we often provide individual help to those who run into difficulty. To remain a Director, you must maintain a minimum unit production figure, or you're in danger of losing the unit. Of course, everything in life is like that—you can't rest on your laurels. "Nothing wilts faster than a laurel rested upon." Not long ago, I got a call from a Director who was desperate. She was in her second month of not making quota, and that meant she was about to lose her unit. She said, "Mary Kay, what can I do?"

I said, "Okay, tell you what. Call your group together in an emergency session, and tell them the facts of what's about to happen. If they really want to remain a unit, they will rally around you. Explain to them that your unit needs $3,000 wholesale this month in order to remain a unit. Then tell them that all they need to do—everyone in the unit—is pledge to sell a Basic Skin Care Set each day, or its equivalent—anyone can do that!"

She did as I suggested at her next sales meeting.

Then she took out a big poster with lines on it, and said, "If you pledge that you will sell a Basic a day for this week, then I want you to come up and put your name on the board." Everyone there went up and signed her pledge.

You see, what she did was take her big problem and set up *small, attainable daily goals.* And she didn't ask them to do anything she didn't do, by the way. She sold her Basic a day, too. At the end of the week, everyone had a gold star by her name, because every single person had made good on her pledge. And the result was that this Director went from not making her $3,000 quota to doing more than $12,000 *in one month.*

That's how you eat an elephant one bite at a time!

When that Director's unit reached $12,000, she had attained what we call "on target" Cadillac status. This is one of our incentive programs which gives people something to work toward. The Cadillac program actually started when I bought a Cadillac in 1966 and decided I wanted it to be Mary Kay pink. The Cadillac dealer couldn't believe it. He said, "Mary Kay, you don't mean that, let me tell you how much it's going to cost you to have it repainted when you don't like it!" But I really wanted pink with a white top and white interior, and that's what I got.

That car was a sensation! Everybody loved it, and Directors kept asking me, "Can we have a pink Cadillac as our top prize?" Richard looked at the figures and decided we could. The next year, our top Sales Director received a pink Cadillac. The second year, we presented five, the third year ten, then twenty. Then we opened it up to the plateau system, which is what I prefer above all. That meant that *everybody* who achieved a certain production level received the use of a pink Cadillac.

Right now, the production for Cadillac status is $36,000 wholesale per quarter for two consecutive quarters, although that will change with inflation. Currently, 469 Sales Directors enjoy Cadillac status.

Once again, "Nothing wilts faster than a laurel rested upon." So we introduced a quota system. The Director wins the Cadillac for two years, and in order to keep it, she must maintain a certain production—or pay a prorated portion of the leasing cost each month. As you can imagine, the quota system is very motivating. Once a Director has driven a pink Cadillac for a year, she'll never drive an old black Ford again! If she maintains her production, she gets a new car every two years.

After a few years, we realized that a lot of Directors were doing a great job but hadn't quite reached Cadillac status. So we instituted the Buick Regal program. It requires $24,000 wholesale production for two consecutive quarters to earn one, and 667 Sales Directors are currently qualified in the Regal program. Guess what the bumper sticker on the pink Buick Regal says? "When I Grow Up, I'm Going to Be a Cadillac." We put that on to remind them that this is not the end, but a step to a bigger goal.

We found that when plateaus are clearly defined, women can set their goals one by one. I'm convinced that a woman can do anything. You have to set goals so that they stretch you a bit—but not so they're unreachable.

≈12≈
And God Created Woman

In my speeches to our Consultants, I have often made the statement that when God made man, He was just practicing— even an artist makes a rough draft first! Actually, I say, when God made the world, He looked down and said, "That's good." Then He made man and looked down and said, "That's pretty good, but I think I could do better—*and so He created woman.*"

I tell them this because I want them to realize how very special they are. I truly believe that a woman can do *anything* she wants to do—if she wants it badly enough, and she's willing to pay the price. I think women are fantastic!

Unfortunately, in our society, little boys and little girls are programmed in two different directions. Little girls are usually programmed from birth to think of themselves as growing up to be mothers and homemakers. The average little boy, on the other hand, is told, "You can do anything." From the time he's born, he knows he's going to grow up to be like daddy. He's going to be a big man and the head of a household. If daddy's a fireman, a company president, or a doctor, the little boy aspires to be one, too. When he goes to school, he might find another role model to follow, since there are many good role models for little boys.

But what role model does a little girl have? Usually her mother is the only role model around. She sees that what little girls do when they grow up is scrub floors and wash dishes and cook meals. She normally *isn't* programmed to be a career person. Instead, she's conditioned to think that the ultimate goal is to marry and have a family—not to be a doctor, an architect, or an attorney. It's no wonder that if she does go to work, she often goes at it with no confidence at all.

Even in this enlightened age, relatively few women are zeroing in on professional careers. Many of them are just dreaming about that "fellow on a white horse." We *know* women have as much ability as men. The problem is that *women* don't know it. They haven't been brought up to believe that they can do anything. They've never been told that they're great. Instead, they're told, "Oh, you can't do that, you're a little girl!" The theme for little girls is, "You can't." But the theme for little boys is, "You *can*. You can do anything." Women need to be told they have wonderful qualities. They need to realize that *they* too can do anything they choose to do.

My mother was a very exceptional woman. She never once said, "You can't" to me. During my first marriage, I realized my long-awaited dream of attending college and took pre-med courses in the days when other mothers were telling their daughters to become nurses. My mother had been a nurse, and she didn't want that for me. At that time nurses were second-class citizens. They were the handmaidens of the doctors; anything the doctors didn't want to do, they delegated to the nurses. So mother said, "I don't want you to be a nurse—be a doctor." It was very unusual at the time for a woman to enter pre-med—I was the only woman in the whole class. And the men wouldn't give me the time of day. They just didn't feel I'd ever make it. As it turned out, they were right, but it wasn't because I was a woman that I didn't go to medical school. It was because I had a greater aptitude for working with people, as the dean of my college finally told me.

There are so many outstanding women in medicine today

that there's no question women can do it. In the past, women weren't supposed to pursue the professions. The same thing was true of careers in business. On the rare occasions when a woman did make it to the executive suites, she had to have far more talent than a man to get there. And while she held a position equal to a man's, her salary was never equal! I've always believed that a woman should be paid on the basis of her ability. I can't believe that God intended for a woman's brain to be worth fifty cents on the dollar. And when I presented ideas to my employers, I resented being told, "Oh, Mary Kay, you're thinking like a woman again!"

At that time, "thinking like a woman" meant there was something *wrong* with your thinking. It's hard to believe now that women were ever willing to accept that idea. But women had been second-class citizens for so long that they were brainwashed to believe that nonsense. The fact is, thinking like a woman can be a tremendous advantage. Women have a special, intuitive quality that most men don't possess. Let me give you an example.

Recently, I was walking through a hotel lobby with two men from our administration staff. We were on our way to a meeting, and every few steps Consultants would stop us (the hotel was crowded with Mary Kay people). We went past two girls who were only talking quietly, and who had made no effort to say anything to us, and suddenly I just stopped.

I went over to them and said, "Is anything wrong? Can we help you?"

Well, it seemed they had lost their admittance badges. (We have so many outsiders who want to attend our major meetings that identification badges have become a necessity.) They were on the verge of tears, standing there in despair, not knowing what to do. We made the necessary arrangements for them and then went on.

As soon as we were out of earshot, one of the men turned to me and said, "That's amazing. How in the world, just walking past those two women, did you know something was wrong?"

"I really don't know," I said. "I just knew something was."

The men couldn't get over the fact that I could take a single quick glance in their direction and realize there was something wrong. But I believe that women can often sense things that most men would never notice.

Our Consultants are often very intuitive, too. Many times they'll understand what a woman means, even though it isn't obvious at all. For instance, suppose a woman has a facial and puts the cosmetics on and just looks terrific, but then she says, "I might buy it some other time." A Consultant will sense that the woman has a reason for not buying that she doesn't want to state. The woman might even say, "I don't really like this," but it's obvious by the way she looks at herself in the mirror that she *does* like it. So a good Consultant will intuitively sense that the woman's real reason for not buying is that she doesn't feel she can afford to. Perhaps the Consultant will say, "You know, why don't you have a Show? Do you realize that by having a Beauty Show of your own, you can earn whatever you want?"

And often the woman immediately acquiesces, because her real problem was that she couldn't afford it. You know she likes the cosmetics, because she was very enthusiastic, and *now* she has a chance to earn what she couldn't afford to buy.

An interesting example of woman's intuition occurred when we first started the company. Before we actually opened our doors, I was recruiting salespeople. You can imagine how much I needed Consultants. I applied the "three-foot rule" to everyone I met. (If they came within three feet of me, I asked them if they wanted to become Consultants!) By the day we opened, I had recruited nine people.

There was one man among them who seemed to have more enthusiasm and more ideas than everyone else put together. He looked like a real winner!

But somehow, on our very first day, I found myself standing out in the mall of Exchange Park saying to him, "I'm sorry, but I just don't think you'll do." It certainly wasn't because he was a man, and I really didn't have a fact to back up my feelings. But my intuition was telling me something was wrong.

Remember, this was our very *first* day in business, and my life's savings were on the line. If the business didn't work out, I would lose everything and have to go back to work for somebody else again. My head was saying, "You idiot! This man has more on the ball than everyone else put together!"

But my heart was saying, "You're right, Mary Kay. There's something wrong here."

The man was absolutely furious with me. He said, "I'll show you. I'll start my own cosmetic business in competition with you!"

I said, "Well, O.K., good luck!"

Six months later, I opened the newspaper to see a front-page story about him. He had been indicted on a felony charge. Had he been a member of our organization, it might have been "our Watergate" before there was one!

Intuition is just one of the special qualities God gave women. Another quality that's very precious is femininity. I truly believe He made us feminine for a reason, and we should retain our femininity. I do believe women should pursue careers if they want to, but I don't think they should ever put their femininity aside. Frankly, I can't see why they should do a lot of the heavy, masculine work that women do in places like Russia. It hurts me to see a woman cleaning streets or working at loading docks. And it worries me to think of a woman wearing a helmet, all messed up and muddy, sitting in a foxhole somewhere with a gun. That just doesn't make any sense to me.

I don't believe women are geared to do things like that—psychologically, physically, or mentally. And I think jobs of that kind are not suitable for women.

Women can become successful without discarding their femininity and behaving like men. It turns me off when I see a woman with a cigarette hanging out of the side of her mouth. And I don't think women should reduce themselves to cursing. I've seen women join in with the profanity when they're around men, and some of them are better at it than men. But I believe men prefer women to act feminine. If a woman does, the men will not even use profanity. I recall one meeting where I was the only woman present, and someone said, "Since you're here, Mary Kay, I guess we will have to clean up our language."

I said, "Gentlemen, I'm happy to be one of you. I will ask or give no quarter; however, if any of you are looking for an excuse to clean up your language, be my guest!" I've always found that when a woman behaves like a lady, she sets the stage, and the men will then conduct themselves as gentlemen.

When I am the only woman present at a meeting, and this happens quite often, I go out of my way to dress extra-attractively that day (even if I am a great-grandmother!). But I find that femininity is a definite asset. I think men respect a woman who retains her femininity, and they respond more favorably to a woman who presents an attractive appearance.

I've also learned that it's wise to keep my mouth shut when I'm at a meeting with all men unless I'm absolutely certain of my ground. (You can look very brilliant with your mouth shut!) As the old saying goes, "It's better to have people wonder why you didn't speak than why you did." So I have found that it's better to wait, and at the right time, when I'm sure of my ideas, to say what I think. Then, the men all listen.

Recently, I talked to a woman who's been in business many years, and she made a very interesting observation. She believes men don't expect as much from a woman in the business world as they do from a man, and that this can be an asset instead of a liability. "A well-groomed saleswoman," she told me, "can often get in to see an executive who would turn a man away. In fact, he's likely to hold the chair for her!" In other words, men will often give a woman a little extra assistance. And a woman who dresses attractively gives herself an even greater edge.

When I stress dressing in an attractive, feminine way, I

don't mean wearing sexy clothes. A career woman should dress in a businesslike manner. Personally, I'm opposed to women wearing pants on the job. In fact, that's a company policy at Mary Kay (except in the manufacturing area). After all, we are in the business of helping women look more feminine and beautiful, so we feel very strongly that our Beauty Consultants should dress accordingly. We suggest they always wear dresses to Shows, rather than pants, and we emphasize well-groomed hair and nails. After all, can you imagine a woman with her hair up in curlers, wearing jeans, calling herself a Beauty Consultant—and trying to tell other women what they should be doing to look good? Those women would have to think, "What in the world can *she* possibly tell me about looking beautiful?" We want our Consultants to be the kind of women other women will want to emulate. We're really selling femininity, so our dress code has to be ultra-feminine.

I believe that whatever kind of work a woman does, it's always to her advantage to look feminine and pretty. It just makes sense to have as much going for you as you can. Not too long ago, I saw a very good example of how important it can be to look good. I had been contacted by a woman (I'll call her Dr. Smith) who was gathering material for a book on self-made American women. Her credentials were very impressive—she had a Ph.D. and had been in business herself. Richard thought the book was a worthwhile idea, so he and I agreed to spend an afternoon with her when she flew in from another state.

I wanted to look like a chairman of the board for the interview, so on the day she was arriving, I wore a black silk suit and diamonds. The interview was scheduled to begin at two. About five minutes before two, I stepped outside my office, and there at my secretary's desk stood this dreadful-looking woman! She was wearing a pair of slacks and a short-sleeved shirt and some sneaker-type shoes. She had a mannish haircut and no makeup, and she really looked like she should have been out gardening. In fact, her fingernails looked like she *had* been out gardening. Well, I knew she couldn't be one of our people, because that sort of dress and grooming is taboo at Mary Kay.

I called Jennifer aside and said, "For heaven's sake, get that woman out of here before Dr. Smith arrives."

Jennifer came back in a moment and said, "Mary Kay, that *is* Dr. Smith."

I couldn't believe it!

She came in and sat down, and we got off to a bad start. She asked me about our company image, and of course I had to talk about how we stress femininity and grooming—which she already knew. But she glanced down at her attire and unkept hands and it was clear we had a difference of opinion.

I was very relieved when Richard walked in. I thought, "Oh, good, the rest of this afternoon is going to go better."

But when he opened the door and glanced at her, he said, "Oh, excuse me," and started to leave. He was sure he had his schedule mixed up. This *couldn't* be the lady Ph.D. we were expecting.

"Oh, Richard, just a moment, please," I called. He came back.

"Richard," I said, "may I present Dr. Smith?" His look told me how amazed he was.

Richard spent all of five minutes with that woman before he politely excused himself. He could have contributed immensely to what she wanted to know, but he was so turned off by her appearance that he didn't give her the time of day. I think there's a good lesson in the way Richard reacted. He had lost his respect for her when he saw how carelessly she was dressed. No matter what a woman does, it's worthwhile to take the time to look the best she can. After all, you only get one chance to make a good first impression.

I think it makes good sense for a woman to try to have everything she can going for her. And an attractive appearance is something every woman can achieve—if she really makes up her mind to do it. Marilyn Kogut, a Future Director out on the West Coast, is a shining example of what a woman can do if she is determined.

Seven years ago, Marilyn's doctor told her she was losing her sight, and would be totally blind within approximately three years. In the process of trying to find some solution, Marilyn and her husband went bankrupt, and lost their home and their business. The only eye surgeon who told her he would operate said there was a fifty-fifty chance; she would either wake up from the operation blind, or she would wake up with her eyesight restored. Marilyn weighed the odds and decided she would rather have her remaining three years of vision than undergo the operation and risk losing her eyesight immediately.

One of Marilyn's concerns about being blind was her appearance. She had been in fashion and modeling all her life, and she was very fastidious about her appearance. The thought of being unable to do her hair and make up her face was unbearable. So she decided she would learn how to do it without sight, while she still could. She practiced and practiced, with her eyes closed. She would open them and check, and then practice again. She worked until she was able to apply her makeup perfectly. She even put her eyeliner on without sight. That was the hardest part, because eyeliner must be very even and delicate. In order to master it, she would refrigerate her eyeliner so she could feel the cold against her eyelids!

Marilyn has been blind for some time now. Many people who first meet her don't know that, and they find it hard to believe. They often ask, "Who does your makeup? Who does your hair?" They're astonished to hear that she does it herself.

Marilyn has brought that same kind of determination to her Mary Kay career. She first heard about us when *60 Minutes* did a segment on Mary Kay in October in 1979. It took her several months to get up the confidence to send a tape to me and ask if I thought she could become a Consultant. I was very impressed with her, but I thought, "How in the world can she do this?" I didn't know how, but my woman's intuition said she could, and her background in fashion and cosmetics was very impressive. Marilyn and her husband were in such dire financial circumstances at the time that she had to decide whether to pay the mortgage on their home or use part of the money to buy her beauty case. She decided to buy the case.

The first week she had that case, Marilyn spent every day marking it in Braille. Her fingers were raw from working on it. But at the end of the week, she could find anything in her case as quickly as anyone else. Nevertheless, her friends told her, "Marilyn, this is absolutely ridiculous. This is beyond your capability, you cannot *do* this. Remember, you're blind!"

Well, nobody could remember that better than Marilyn.

But at the end of her very first Show, she had $110 in sales, two bookings for other Shows, and two recruits! It was an amazing first Show. And she went right on from there. If you ask her, Marilyn will tell you she gives God all the credit for everything she's accomplished. And she likes to use my expression, "When God closes a door, He always opens a window."

I began this chapter by saying that women are special, and can do anything they really want to. Marilyn now has eleven recruits, and is on her way to becoming a Director. She still has to depend on her family and friends to drive her to Shows, but she's looking forward to changing that! "When I reach Cadillac status," she told me, "I'm going to hire a driver to take me to shows and dress her all in pink!"

Naturally, I realize that Marilyn is an exceptional woman, and perhaps only one blind person in ten thousand would have the background and skills to do what she's done. But she certainly illustrates that a woman can do anything she makes up her mind to do. Some great person said, "Show me someone who has made it big—and I'll show you someone who shouldn't have made it at all!" God gave women special qualities. But I think because of this, He also requires more of us. Everything that a woman touches should be ennobled.

⌦ 13 ⌫

Getting into the Job Market

More women are working outside the home today than ever before in history. For some families, inflation makes a second income an absolute necessity, while changing life styles have helped many women feel free to pursue careers. Often there are personal reasons a woman decides to go to work. When her children are grown and out of the house, she may no longer feel needed. The nest is empty. She suddenly finds time on her hands. Community work, bridge clubs, the country club, and coffee-klatsches are not enough. She needs something else to occupy her time so that she feels she's doing something worthwhile. A career is often the answer.

Regardless of her reason for doing it, getting into the job market can be a traumatic experience if she's not prepared. This is especially true if she has spent the past twenty years or more as a mother and a homemaker.

Now, I must confess that I don't have any firsthand experience with going to work after a long time at home. I've worked steadily since I was a very young woman. And when I conceived of my dream company in 1963, I had only been retired for a month. But throughout the years, I've had a great deal of experience as an employer, helping thousands of women enter the job market in our corporate office and in the sales force. So with that in mind, I'd like to offer my thoughts to those of you who are thinking about a new career.

Any good homemaker has dozens and dozens of skills that she has developed over the years in the course of doing her job as a wife and mother. Unfortunately, these skills are not usually in great demand in the job market. Furthermore, job experience from twenty years ago is not always applicable in today's working world, especially if you haven't used your skills in the meantime. The fact that you could type sixty or seventy words a minute *then* won't do you much good *now*. I always suggest that a woman take the time to sharpen her skills. They will come back quickly enough, but it does take some practice. Some skills, like taking shorthand, can be practiced at home, with books and records from the public library. You can also take refresher courses. Every city and town of any size has a community college offering these courses. The important thing is to take action to prepare yourself, so you go into that interview feeling confident that you have something to offer.

You also have to realize that *it's your job to sell yourself* to a prospective employer. There are a lot of other women out there competing for the same job. You have to give yourself an "edge" by thinking about what you have to offer the company. So many people who apply for jobs come in asking, "What can the company do for me?" instead of "What can I do for the company?" And sometimes that attitude is the reason they don't get the job. The first thing *you* have to do is ask yourself, "What skills do I have that this company needs? What can I bring them that they don't already have?" The place to start is by taking an inventory of *yourself!* What are your assets? What do you do well? What do you really want to do? If it's what you like and not just a job, you'll be enthusiastic. Put it down in black and white. Until you actually commit it to writing, you're likely to be fuzzy about what you can actually do. On paper, your abilities will become very clear. Don't forget that you have other valuable assets to offer besides your skills. You might write down, "I'm attractive. I like to work with people. I'm outgoing. I'm energetic. I'm determined." Once you put it all on paper, I'm sure you'll discover that you have some wonderful qualities that make *you* a very special person!

An employer has to feel that you have something special to offer, and that you really *want* to work for the company—you're motivated by something *more* than the paycheck. I suggest that before you go job hunting, you sit down and make another list, of all the companies you really like and feel you would like to be a part of. I believe it's important that you think the company you work for is just super. That attitude will do wonders for your morale. During the Christmas season, I receive cards by the score from our people, telling me, "I've never been happier with my work than I have since I joined Mary Kay." Choose a company you feel this way about. Then, when you go in for the interview, your enthusiasm is going to be a big selling factor.

When you've decided on a company, do your homework on that company. You should know a lot about it before you go for the interview. Nothing is more flattering to an interviewer than for a person to come in saying, "I have read about you, I admire this company, and I want to work for you!" When our company was still young, an applicant presented a beautiful résumé with *a list of what he could do to help our company.* At the time, we didn't have an opening for someone with his talents. So he came back the next year. For four straight years, he submitted his résumé and his list of what *he* could do for *us.* Finally we grew to the size where we could use someone with his talents, and we were able to hire him. His ingenuity has saved us countless thousands of dollars over the years! I'm sure other people applied in the meantime who wanted a position like that—but he had done his homework and he was enthusiastic. That makes a candidate very attractive.

Each time you prepare for a job interview, you must tell yourself that this prospective employer is going to say yes. But you also have to know that there's a possibility that won't happen. Only about one in ten job interviews results in a job. It's very much like selling. A top salesperson knows he or she won't close every sale, but it's necessary to believe that *this* one will result in a sale! So go into each interview thinking, "This is going to be the one who says yes." But recognize that you may not be accepted, and then rejection won't come so bitterly. If you are turned down, then say to yourself, "I'm that much closer to finding a company where I will be an asset." With this attitude, it's just a matter of time until you find the position you want.

Before an interview, make sure your appearance is in order. Remember that saying: "You only get one chance to make a good *first* impression!" As far as dress is concerned, I think a suit is most appropriate for a job interview. You want to look like a professional businesswoman. Forget about anything with frills, and *don't* go in wearing something sexy. More than likely, you'll be interviewed by a woman, anyway, so keep that in mind when you consider what to wear. If you *feel* well-dressed, it will give you added confidence, as well as making a good impression. Just *knowing* you look your best will do wonders!

Before you actually go to work, I think it's wise to ask yourself, "Who's going to do all the things at home that I do now?" This is an important consideration, especially if you have small children who must be cared for. A baby sitter or day nursery cannot do for the children *all* the things that need to be done. And don't forget, the housework will still be there. If you won't be able to hire a housekeeper when you go to work, I suggest you make a few trial runs at "How fast can I get this work done?" You need to know whether you're going to be able to manage a job and do the housework. Knowing how much time your homemaking takes can help you decide what position is right for you.

It's also important to think about the *cost* of working before you make a decision. For instance, if you have to pay for a baby sitter or day nursery, that will be a considerable expense. Then you must figure transportation, what it costs you to go to and from work. If public transportation isn't available, parking will cost money, too. In large downtown areas, parking currently costs $40 a month or more. In midtown Manhattan, forget it—you'd have to hock your car to pay for the parking. If you drive to work, parking is just one expense. You'll also have gasoline expenses, maintenance, and the cost of the car payments.

Another expense that you must figure is clothing. If you work downtown, you'll need nice clothes, and a different outfit for every day of the week. No woman wants to wear the same thing day in and day out. And those clothes will usually require dry cleaning, another expense you could have avoided by staying home. There will be the cost of hair styling, and perhaps manicures. And you're probably going to be eating lunch out. Have you paid attention to the cost of lunch in a downtown restaurant lately? Even a fast-food lunch is $3—and nobody can eat a hamburger every day. Coffee breaks can be expensive, too. If you just get a Coke or a cup of coffee out of a vending machine, it can be fifty cents. Snacks, such as a candy bar or some potato chips, could add another dollar a day.

Add to all this the fact that your income will probably push your husband into a higher tax bracket, and sometimes it works out that a woman's husband is *paying* to have her away from home! So, from a financial point of view, unless you can keep your expenses down, you might be better off *not* entering the work force. I've seen projections in which a woman totaled all her expenses and found that instead of "making $150 a week" she actually was bringing home a grand total of twenty-three cents an hour!

When a woman enters our business, her husband often takes these expenses into consideration, and says, "How much is this new little hobby going to cost me?" Most men aren't upset by the initial beauty case investment of $75. In some cases, they even think, "Okay, so she's going to fool around with this Mary Kay thing. It'll keep her busy and out of the department stores." In other instances, a woman who decides to start her own business such as a dress shop will have to make a substantial investment—many times, literally tens of thousands of dollars.

Women who have been out of the job market for many years and don't know where to look for employment sometimes think, "Well, I'll just start my own business." Too often they're not aware of the tremendous odds against them, let alone the problems a business owner faces every single day. In the cosmetic field, for instance, I'm told that thousands of companies spring up every year. In fact, many of these started because somebody saw how Mary Kay Cosmetics had succeeded, and thought cosmetics must be an easy business to launch. A few months later, sadly, they're out of business. There can be any one of a million reasons they failed.

Many businesses fail because they're undercapitalized in the beginning. I think it's important to note that while we started with $5,000 paid in capital, it would take much more than that now. And, even if you do have enough money to invest, that's no guarantee of success.

Obviously, it takes more than money to make a new business succeed. You really must know what you're doing. And you've got to remember that there's a lot of competition. Unless you really can "build a better mousetrap," there's not much reason for anyone to beat a path to your door.

Only a small percentage of new businesses do succeed. I think one reason for that is that people go into a business simply because they *want* to be in that business. That's not a good enough reason. A woman may love decorating her own home, so she thinks, "Gee, I want to be an interior decorator." The community probably already has skilled, well-established decorators. Many women want to go into the glamour professions, like fashion, without any real training or experience. It is not wise to start a business unless you have something new or different or better to offer than is presently being offered.

The best reason to start a new company is that *there is a need for what you have to offer,* or that you're better than what is being offered. When we began, no cosmetic company was actually teaching skin care. All of them were just selling rouge or lipstick or new eye colors. No company was teaching women how to care for their skin. So we came into a market where there was a real need—and we filled it. Oddly enough, it's still true today that women are not knowledgeable about skin care, despite all the information on television, in magazines, and in newspapers. They buy a product here, there, and everywhere, but they don't have a coordinated program. We fill a void by helping women understand how to take care of their skin. So, if you want to start a successful business, you must offer something different or something better than what is available.

Women have so many talents that they never attempt to use. If you want to start your own business, ask yourself what you really *do well,* something that makes people say to you, "If you ever decide to go into business, you should bake bread. This bread is the *best* I've ever eaten!" Some of the most successful new businesses around were started by women working out of their own homes, using their special talents. Working out of the home keeps overhead to a minimum, and that can often make the difference in whether an enterprise succeeds or fails. There are tax advantages, too, and if you decide to start a cottage industry, be sure to get a competent accountant's advice.

Many women have succeeded with small businesses they started right in their own kitchens or garages. I know of one woman who had a fruitcake recipe her great-grandmother had given her. She began her enterprise by selling a few homemade fruitcakes at Christmas time. Now her business is a huge industry, making and selling thousands of wonderful fruitcakes each Christmas! (Despite the growth of her business, now employing about a hundred people each fall, the fruitcakes are *still* mixed by hand because she feels this controls her quality.) Her company is Mary of Puddin' Hill.

Another woman, with a real skill in making draperies and slipcovers, began here in Dallas as a neighborhood seamstress. That venture has also grown into a large business. One woman who runs a very successful infants' shop started by making baby clothes for her grandchildren. Still another woman decided when she was pregnant that she didn't like the ugly maternity dresses available, and began designing better ones. She saw a need and filled it. Betty Graham thought there had to be a better way to correct typing errors, and she experimented in her kitchen until she came up with Liquid Paper. Before she died, the company she began was sold for more than $40 million!

One of my favorite success stories is about Mary Crowley, who owns Home Interiors & Gifts, one of the most successful direct sales organizations in the country. I especially enjoy telling about Mary because she and I have had such an influence on each other's lives.

I met Mary in the early 1940s, when I was with Stanley Home Products. It was a bitterly cold night, when the streets were sheeted with ice and the radio was warning people not to leave their homes—but I had a Stanley party scheduled. I was conscientious, and if I had a party booked, I went. So I did.

Well, Mary Crowley was very conscientious, too—and she was the only other person who came. As the Sunday School teacher of the hostess, she felt an obligation to keep her commitment—and not even that terrible weather could stop Mary. I quickly realized there was no point in trying to put on a demonstration just for her and the hostess, so I decided to just enjoy the cake and coffee and the good company. Both women were lovely people. And Mary was an exciting personality. She really had charisma.

As we talked, I discovered that she worked as secretary to the president of the Purse Manufacturing Company. This was before the freeways had been built in Dallas, and getting downtown and back every day seemed to be a real problem for her. I mentioned to her that I was able to arrange my working day to avoid rush-hour traffic, and that seemed to impress her. Like me, she had young children at home, and the fact that I could be home by four in the afternoon interested her, too.

After we were better acquainted, I asked her how much she earned as secretary to the president. She looked at me as if it was really none of my business (and it wasn't), and she said, "I make sixty-six dollars a week." In those days, that was a lot of money.

I said, "Well, I do too—in a bad week." *That* impressed her, too. But when I offered her a job as a Stanley dealer, she said no.

I told her, "You would be fantastic in sales. You're wasting your time behind a desk. All I can say is that if you ever change your mind, call me."

I didn't hear from her for over a month, and then one day she phoned to tell me her husband had been called up for reserve duty in the National Guard for three months. "So I'm going to be home alone," she said. "Do you think I could sell Stanley part time?"

Usually I had little interest in part-timers, but remembering Mary's wonderful personality, I consented. The first party I took her to was a disaster! I made a total of $4. But it didn't bother her. I took her on a few more parties, and the first thing you knew she had her case and went to work. And she was terrific!

After a few months, she called and told me she would be at the Monday morning sales meeting. She had resigned her job and was going to sell Stanley full time! Well, that was the beginning of something wonderful for me, because from then on, whatever I couldn't think of, she did. My unit soared to the top with her assistance.

Later, when I moved to St. Louis, Mary had done such a fantastic job that Stanley allowed her to take over my Dallas unit. She was earning tremendous commissions with this, but she had a personality conflict with the sales manager. About six months later, when she was offered a job as sales manager of World Gift, a brand-new, fledgling company, she saw a big future in the company, and took the position.

A year later, we moved back to Houston, and I came through Dallas. While I was there, Mary took me to a World Gift show—and this time *she* recruited *me*. I took my World Gift case to Houston and started my business there. And within a year, my unit in Houston was doing a major portion of the company's total business!

Some time after this, Mary left World Gift to start her own company, Home Interiors & Gifts. Today, her company is doing several hundred million dollars a year in retail sales!

Mary influenced my life in many ways, but one of the most important was that she introduced me to Mel, my late husband. He was in the wholesale gift business at the time, and one day he was in her office. He had only been in Dallas a few months, and because he traveled so much, he hadn't had a chance to make many friends. He invited Mary and her husband, Dave, out to dinner. And he said, "Do you know anybody else like you?"

Mary said, "As a matter of fact, I do," and she picked up the phone and called me. I was a little reluctant, but I agreed to dinner the next evening with them. The next day around five, she called again and told me something had come up and she and Dave couldn't go! I suspected her of playing Cupid right then, but I agreed to go. And that's how I met Mel.

Isn't it wonderful how, once in a while, someone crosses your path who turns out to have a dramatic influence on your life? And to think that I never would have met Mary if we hadn't both gone to that Stanley party on that cold winter night!

In my mind, Mary is a wonderful example of how a Christian woman who uses her talents *can* be a success in anything she makes up her mind to do. Mary was an excellent secretary, then a top salesperson, and later an outstanding sales manager. Then she started a small business which grew into a large company. Remember: "Huge oaks from little acorns grow."

A woman who starts her own company, or for that matter becomes an independent saleswoman, is her own boss. If she's going to be successful, she has to work for the most exacting boss in the world—herself. I often admonish our Consultants, "You must discipline yourself to work as if you were working for someone else." That means you must set aside exact hours to work every day. Ask yourself, "How many hours a day *can* I spend on my work?" Once you have made the decision, *no matter what happens,* you must stick to those hours. Early in my sales career, I decided that at eight-thirty every morning I would begin work on something that had to do with my job. When I figured the value of my time—on straight commission—I knew I couldn't afford to stop for coffee breaks half a dozen times a day. I've known people, whose time was valued at $25 or $50 an hour, who took half-hour coffee breaks every morning. At that rate, those breaks are costing a lot more than the price of a cup of coffee! Employers really appreciate employees who value time. You may think they don't notice—but they do.

So, as you can see, if you decide to enter the job market, there are a great many things to consider. You may want to risk investing money in a business venture. You may want the security of a salaried position. However, your *security* is sometimes jeopardized by whether or not your employer likes you and the way you do things. When I first went to work, I was attracted to the flexible hours of commissioned sales. I also liked the idea that I controlled my earnings, which I certainly couldn't do in a salaried job. And I knew I didn't want to be away from the children for eight or ten hours each day. And, in those days, I really wasn't qualified to do anything other than be a clerk in a retail store. And then the pay was something like $1.50 a day for eight hours on your feet!

I really believe the *only difference* between successful people and unsuccessful people is extraordinary determination! If you see a woman doing something you would like to do, ask yourself, "What has she got that I can't have fixed?" In other words, "How can I do it, too?" I believe any woman can be successful if she has *enough determination*. One of my favorite quotes is, "If you aren't happy with yourself, climb back up on God's easel. He's not through with you yet."

Although I was a young woman when I started my sales career, don't forget that I had retired before I founded Mary Kay Cosmetics. So if you're not satisfied with your status quo, it's never too late. After all, it took God a long time to get me ready for the job that He had for me.

～14～
Looking Good and Feeling Great

Sometimes a woman will come to a Beauty Show and literally sit there with her arms folded and say, "I'm too old, I'm too ugly, and there's nothing you can do about it. I'm hopeless." We usually gently coax and persuade a woman like that: "Your face will feel so soft and nice, I know you'll enjoy it, please try!"

If the Consultant is tactful enough, the woman will usually consent to have a facial. Then, when her skin looks and feels better, she'll agree to try the Day Radiance, and then a little of the Glamour makeup. An hour later, the Consultant will find it difficult to pry the mirror from the woman's hands—because she suddenly feels *pretty*. And it's obvious that she feels prettier *inside*, too. It's experiences like this that make our business so rewarding.

When a woman sits down in front of a mirror with that little palette, and changes from an ugly duckling to a swan, it's like watching a miracle happen! The difference is so striking. And somehow a woman feels like she looks. When she looks pretty, she radiates self-esteem. She goes home with her head held high and she even seems to walk differently. I think the experience is similar to how we all feel when we leave the beauty salon with a new hair style.

It's no wonder that cosmetics are said to be one of the

three depression-proof industries, along with beer and cigarettes. During the Great Depression, beer was obviously a cheap way to console yourself. And people smoked to ease their tension. As for cosmetics, when times are bad, a woman perhaps can't afford to buy a new dress, but she *can* get a lift by buying a new lip color. In fact, her spirits could be lifted more by a purchase of cosmetics than by going out to lunch.

It's a known fact that looking pretty makes a woman *feel* better. Take the case of a woman who has been seriously ill. When the doctor comes in one day and finds she has done something about her hair, and put on a little lip color and a touch of makeup, he knows that she's on her way back.

It's amazing what cosmetics can do for a woman. I'll never forget one incident that occurred during the very early days of the company. We were running ads to recruit people in Sherman, Texas and operating out of a motel there. We advertised that we would give a complimentary facial as a way of introducing our new product, which in turn could be recommended in the community. The response to the ad was poor. Then at four, it was announced on the radio that a very bad snowstorm was under way.

"Let's pack up and leave," I said, "or we're going to get snowed in." So we began hurriedly packing, but just then the phone rang. It was a woman who sounded better than anyone I had talked to all day. She said she lived just a few blocks away, so I told her to come right over, as quickly as possible because we were about to leave.

The Sales Director who was with me was very unhappy with this new development, because she wanted to get back to Dallas before the roads became any more hazardous. I told her how good the woman sounded—she was the best of the day! And I added, "I hate to leave without having found anyone here."

So we put everything out again, and in a few minutes there was a knock at the door, I went to answer it, and there stood the most gargantuan woman I have ever seen. She was at least six foot six. She had on a pair of tight black pants—and her end did not justify her jeans! With them, she was wearing a black turtleneck sweater, and on her hair a black snood, one of those old-fashioned crocheted nets that women sometimes used to cover up a "hair don't." And no eye makeup at all!

I could just see my Sales Director thinking, with her raised eyebrows, "The best of the day? Hmmm." This woman didn't fit the picture at all.

But we had promised a facial in the ad. So I asked the Sales Director to give the woman a facial while I went over to the office and checked out. She began by giving this woman the fastest facial in the world, complete with makeup.

At that time in our early history, we were still selling wigs, too. So, as a finishing touch, she plopped a lovely blond wig on the woman's head. This wig had looked gorgeous on the mannequin, but had been at least two inches too large for anyone else. But for her—it was perfect! I want you to know that you've never seen such a transformation in your life! She actually looked beautiful!

When I returned, that woman was sitting in front of the mirror with tears in her eyes. And she said, "This is the first time in my whole life I've ever been pretty."

The woman had told me on the telephone that her husband had been out of work for some time and how much she loved him and her two children and how good she would feel if she could help him. They were pretty bad off financially, and probably the only thing of any value she had was a gold ring. She took off her ring and looked up at me and said, "Mary Kay, would you let me go home and let my husband see me looking like this just once? I'll give you my ring as security." Of course, you know I let her wear that wig home.

We drove to Dallas through that snowstorm, but the feeling I had seeing her joy made it all worthwhile. When we arrived in Dallas, Richard told me that was the last time I could ever take chickens or pigs or rings in exchange for merchandise.

A tremendous change comes over a woman when she's looking good and knows it. A woman's psychology is such that when she looks attractive, she becomes more confident. And when she *doesn't* look good, she doesn't *feel good* about herself. Suppose a woman is in the middle of baking a cake and discovers she's out of cinnamon. She's in jeans, her hair is rolled up, her face isn't made up, and she knows she looks terrible. But she must have that cinnamon, so she decides to dash down to the neighborhood grocery store to get it. Invariably she'll meet someone she didn't want to see, and it's awfully difficult to hide behind those tomato cans.

But let's say that same woman is on the way home from a wedding, knowing she looks her very best. If she meets someone then, she'll have an entirely different attitude. She'll radiate confidence. There's no question that a woman who looks prettier on the outside will feel prettier on the inside, too.

Some years ago, I was holding a training class in Houston. One of the Consultants in the class had never had a $100 Show. She had been with the company about three months, and she had been to one training class after another, but somehow success seemed to be eluding her.

In talking to this class, I said, "You know, you must feel confident. Before your Beauty Show, do your hair and your nails. And if you don't have a dress that makes you feel like a million dollars, go buy one." (I had no idea of the effect that statement would have on her.) "If you have just one dress in your closet that makes you feel terrific, one that wins compliments for you, wear that dress to every Show until you can afford to by a second one."

This woman and her husband had been enduring severe financial difficulties, and she hadn't *had* a new dress for years. But she left that training class and went directly out and bought a new dress. That night, she had her first $100 Show.

Well! She was so excited! She decided that if a new dress was the answer, before her second Show of that week she'd go buy another one. And she did. That evening, she had a second

$100 Show! She did the same thing for her third Show the next day, and had still another $100 Show. She had bought three new dresses and had three $100 Shows! On Monday morning, she came to a sales meeting and announced, "I've got the secret. I've found it! The secret is to buy a new dress."

Of course, that wasn't the secret at all. The secret was that at long last she was confident that she looked good. And, with her new self-confidence, she was able to project more enthusiasm and conviction in her presentation. This explains why some of our Consultants have what they call a "lucky" dress, a certain dress that always seems to make a Show go better. It's really a state of mind. But you'll hear quite often: "Every time I wear my red dress, I have a $200 Show!"

Frequently a woman will come into our organization who reminds me of a tight little rosebud, and it always amazes me how she "blossoms" in a short period of time. Often, when a woman first joins our company, she may not know how to dress. But invariably she will want to "fit in" with the women around her. The first thing you know, she undergoes a change, not only in the way she dresses, but in how she looks and how she takes care of herself. She becomes a more attractive woman. This happens constantly. Generally, a woman who is not well-groomed when she comes into our organization will soon "shape up or ship out," since all of us like to "fit in" with our peers. It reminds me of children in school. If everyone is wearing jeans and some little girl is made to wear a dress, she will feel uncomfortable because she doesn't fit in with the other children.

I've talked about how important it is for women to look good, but I think men care just as much about their appearance. However, unfortunately, often you'll see a man dressed in beautiful clothes, with good-looking shoes, an expensive briefcase, well-groomed hair, and manicured nails—but whose face could look so much better with a little help! If you go back in history, there have been times when men did use makeup and wear wigs. A woman wouldn't look complete without her face made up. So why shouldn't a man do the same thing?

More and more I'm beginning to think that the day may come when men *will* use makeup. We seem to be heading in that direction. Just glance in a barber salon and take a look at all the men lined up under the hair dryers. And if they can enhance their looks by practicing good skin care, why not?

Perhaps the only thing that prevents men from using makeup is the fact that in the past it has been considered effeminate. But then, there was a time not long ago when it was considered effeminate for a man to smoke a filter cigarette. Marlboro changed that, with their commercial that showed macho men smoking filters. And, in an area more closely related to the cosmetic business, not thirty years ago it was considered effeminate for men to use deodorant. But today, the "he-man" smell is no longer in favor. I don't think it's unreasonable to expect to see men using makeup someday in the not too distant future. After all, they enjoy looking their best, too.

When we first began our company, it wasn't long before we noticed many women reordering Basic Skin Care Sets much sooner than we expected. We were concerned because we wanted to be certain our customers were following the correct usage procedure, so we would call and say, "Let's review how you are using the Masque and the Night Cream, etc. You may be overdoing it. You shouldn't have used your Basic Set in just a month."

After a few minutes of conversation, the woman would finally admit that the reason she had used it so quickly was that her husband was using it, too. She would explain that he had seen how great she looked, and she had convinced him to try this product. And behind closed doors, he would have his facial out of her pink jars.

After several such incidents, we decided to introduce our Mr. K line. I felt men would feel foolish using something out of a pink jar labeled Mary Kay, so we designed a masculine package and changed the labels. "Night Cream" became "moisture balm" and "Cleansing Cream" became "cleanser," etc. The men's line comes in masculine brown-and-silver tubes and is packaged conveniently in a handsome tote bag that can be packed in travel kits. Since we seldom have men attending Beauty Shows, Mr. K is almost always purchased by women for their husbands or boyfriends. Actually, it only accounts for a small percentage of our sales, but that represents quite a few loyal customers.

People are often surprised that we have a successful line for men. But then, you might not think elderly women in nursing homes would be interested in cosmetics, either. Yet I found that every time I visited my mother in her nursing home in Houston, she would say, "Oh, honey, did you bring your beauty case?" Of course, I always did. And she'd ask, "Darling, would you fix my face?"

Each time I made Mother up, everyone in the nursing home told her how pretty she looked, and even in her eighties she really enjoyed that. After I made up her face, I would do her hair, and she would put on a pretty dress and go out of her room to see her friends. She just loved that. She got such a good reaction that the woman who shared her room asked one day if I would give her a facial, too. So I did, and she received the same compliments.

"Hmm," I thought, "wouldn't it be wonderful if one day a week Mother could invite six of her friends, and a Houston Consultant could come out and give them facials—strictly as a goodwill gesture? It would be something for these women to look forward to."

At a meeting of the Houston Consultants and Sales Directors, I submitted my idea, and pointed out that there were fifty-five Consultants in attendance that day, so that if each Consultant would go out just once, a Beauty Show could be given each week of the year.

Everybody agreed that it was a great idea, and that it would help these elderly people feel so much better about themselves. The Consultants knew they would not make any money from these Shows, but it would be a good deed. So I scheduled the first Beauty Show for the nursing home on the following Tuesday, and since my daughter, Marylyn, was a Sales Director in Houston, I asked her to be the first to go, so her grandmother would feel more comfortable. When I told Mother about it, she was very excited. It gave her a chance to give something to the other people and she immediately invited six women for the next Tuesday.

Marylyn arrived at the appointed time, and she gave Mother's friends their facials. They absolutely loved it. What she *didn't* anticipate was that they would buy the products. They ordered $156 in merchandise! After that, a Mary Kay Consultant went back each week and gave a Beauty Show. The first thing you knew, almost all the women in the nursing home were using Mary Kay Cosmetics—because using them not only made them look better, it made them feel better, too.

A few years later, our company was able to participate in a scientifically documented experiment at the Golden Acres Nursing Home in Dallas to prove that looking good makes people feel better. My doctor, Herman Kantor, called one evening and asked if he could come over. When he arrived, his wife was with him. They explained that he was on the board of directors of the Golden Acres Nursing Home, and they wanted to do an experiment there to determine whether it was true that a woman who looked better would feel better. Dr. Kantor explained, "We decided that, because of the way Mary Kay conducts skin care classes and improves women's self-images, there was no better company in the world to take part in this experiment." He explained that the entire program would be monitored and evaluated by a team of doctors, including a psychiatrist and psychologist.

There were some 350 residents in the home at that time. The researchers felt they needed at least sixty volunteers in order to have a large enough number to monitor the results. At first, it was difficult to interest the women. They would say, "Honey, you're twenty years too late." We found people just sitting motionless in front of the television set, most of them asleep. They seemed to have little zest for life. It was very depressing.

Finally we did persuade sixty women, and we trained the volunteers who would be coming in at seven each morning to help them with their daily routine and their makeup. The program commenced.

Two months later, I went to see how things were progressing. It was absolutely amazing! I found women with their makeup on, dressed in their best clothes and wearing jewelry as if they were going to church that morning. I couldn't get over the change.

In the beginning, the men hadn't been included in the program, because nobody thought a seventy- or eighty-year-old man would be interested. But as I went through the nursing home, at least half a dozen men came up to me and said, "We demand equal rights!" They wanted to be in the program, too!

At the end of the six months, the program was a documented success. A tremendous change had occurred. Women were getting up early in the morning and saying, "Where's my volunteer?" Somebody would have to explain that the volunteer wasn't due to arrive until later. At the end of the program, the home invited me to a luncheon in my honor. They wanted to show their gratitude. Everyone was dressed up, alert looking, and bright eyed. The transformation was almost unbelieveable. I was so touched.

After the luncheon, Dr. Kantor's wife, who had spearheaded the program, said to me, "Mary Kay, there is one person who couldn't come to the luncheon, but it would really please you to see her. Would you come upstairs with me?"

She took me to a ward I had seen when I first toured the home six months before. This was where they placed people with serious mental problems. I remember one particular woman vividly. She had completely lost her ability to reason.

She was like a child, and so slight that she sat in a child's highchair. That was where they kept her during the day, secured, so she wouldn't fall and hurt herself. She had sat there for three years, day after day, with her head down on the tray, and in all that time she had not shown any awareness of the world around her. She hadn't spoken a word or recognized anyone. I did know that they had decided to include her in the experiment. As we walked upstairs, Mrs. Kantor explained to me that each morning the volunteer would have to hold this lady's head up to put her makeup on. The volunteer would speak soothingly to her, and after she finished, she'd gently put the woman's head back down on the tray. And there she would stay for the rest of the day.

We went through the ward and came to this little lady in her high chair, and Mrs. Kantor stopped. She said, "Dear, this is Mary Kay. This is the lady who has given you your cosmetics every day."

With that, the little lady actually raised her head and looked up, and a faint smile flickered over her face—the first reaction she had shown in three years. As far as I was concerned, that faint flicker of a smile made the whole program worthwhile.

I think what happened at that nursing home illustrates that it's really true—looking good does make people feel better. And I believe that at Mary Kay Cosmetics we are in the business of helping women create better self-images so they will feel better about themselves. That's our contribution to the world. I have often said, "We're not only in the cosmetics business—we're in the people business."

❧ 15 ❧
Happiness Is...

I suppose everyone has his or her own definition of happiness. After all, as the song says, "Happiness is different things to different people." I'd like to share my formula with you. To me, happiness is, first, having work that you love to do—something you like so much you'd do it even if you weren't paid! Second, someone to love. And third, having something to look forward to.

Contrary to many people's thoughts, happiness is *not* guaranteed by money. Very often people who are preoccupied with financial problems think money will solve everything. Of course, money is important—until you have enough of it! By this, I mean enough to support your family in a comfortable manner—good food on the table, adequate clothes, a nice home, and some of the luxuries we have all come to feel are necessities, such as television and automobiles. It's true that it's hard to be happy if you don't have enough money to live comfortably. But once you reach a certain point, money becomes less and less important.

Perhaps you're thinking, "Well, Mary Kay doesn't have to worry about money. She's the chairman of the board of a large company." Yes, that's true—today. But I wasn't always in this position. I know very well from firsthand experience what it's like to live from one commission check to another. I've already

talked about the early days in my career, when I had to produce sales or I couldn't pay my rent at the end of the month.
For many years, I was the sole provider for my three children.
And I can assure you, that responsibility is something I will
never forget. So I can readily identify with someone who's
struggling to make ends meet.

Although I knew financial hardship, there was only one
time in my life when money became a top priority to me. That
was when I began saving to buy our first house. I started with
nothing, and every week I put a few dollars in my savings
account. I still remember how thrilled I was when I finally hit
the $100 mark! Then my goal was to add another zero to that.
When I did, I was on cloud nine. I did all kinds of things to
avoid spending money so that account could grow. And it
took years to accumulate enough to buy my own house.

Money for its own sake has never been tremendously important to me, though. I've heard people say that for them,
money is a way of keeping score. Once they're past a comfortable income, they want to earn more to measure their achievement. They say it's not the money that excites them, but the
idea that they're doing a good enough job to be worth what
they are accumulating.

Of course, different things motivate each of us. But I firmly believe that the happiest people are not the ones with the
most money, but the ones who really enjoy their work. When
our company became a publicly owned corporation in 1968, I
became a millionaire. That poor little girl from the wrong side
of the tracks in Houston had finally made it! But I didn't
think, "Wow, I'm a millionaire! *Now* I'm happy." I realized
that the real thrill was in being able to do the work I loved.
Even today, I get up at five and start on my list of the "six
most important things I must do today." I love the sense of
accomplishment that I feel when at the end of the day that list
is completed. But I don't do it for the money. I haven't worked
for money in a long time. I've often said that I enjoy what I do
so much that I would work for nothing!

Having work you love to do is an essential part of my happiness formula. I truly feel sorry for all the people in this world who go to jobs each morning that they hate. Stop and think about it for a moment. Out of each twenty-four-hour day, you work eight hours, sleep eight hours, then you only have eight hours left. That means your eight-hour workday is equal to your remaining non-sleeping hours. If you are miserable at work, it's bound to affect the rest of your life.

An interesting article I read some time ago said that mental institutions are filled with people who hated what they had done for a living. After years of getting up in the morning and forcing themselves to go to jobs they disliked, one day they simply snapped. Therefore, I feel that to be happy you must love your work. If you hate those eight hours every day, everything else is bound to be colored by that misery.

Many of the women in our company have written to tell me that their success with Mary Kay has made it possible for their husbands to give up jobs they thoroughly disliked and get into fields they really enjoyed. Often the husbands themselves write to tell me how grateful they are. So many of them had felt saddled with the responsibility for their families, and until their wives' incomes as Consultants or Directors made it possible for them to chance starting their own businesses or going into other fields more to their liking, they had felt "locked in." When a Consultant tells me she has earned enough to give her husband this freedom, her shining face makes it clear that nothing could be more satisfying to her.

Of course, the basis of our whole philosophy at Mary Kay has always been that it's better to give than to receive. At the very beginning of her training, a Consultant is told, "Your job is not to sell cosmetics. Your job is to go to a Beauty Show asking yourself, 'What can I do to send these people home feeling more beautiful on the outside, knowing full well that they'll become more beautiful on the inside, too?' " Every Consultant is taught that her job is to give. We have the same emphasis throughout the organization. A Director is told never to look at a Consultant and think, "Gee, she can produce X dollars in commissions for me this month." Instead, the Director must think about how she can help a Consultant reach within herself and bring out the talent that she never even tried to use. In our business, we get happiness by giving. As someone once said, "Flowers leave their fragrance on the hand which bestows them."

Today, I would say that one of the things that gives me the most happiness is seeing how many of our people love *their* work at Mary Kay. I often receive letters that say, "I love being a Consultant so much, I'd do it for free!" It's a great joy to me to know how many other women in our company share my feelings.

When you enjoy your work this much, it's important to have someone to share it with. Without that somebody, you can be the most successful person in the world, but your happiness somehow is not complete. Think of how many people with glamorous, high-paying work have not found happiness. Marilyn Monroe is a good example. On the surface, she had everything. She was beautiful and wealthy, and had an exciting career. Yet, at the height of her fame, she took her own life. It was hard to understand how someone in her position could have been so miserable. After her death, though, people who had known her revealed how lonely she had been. I think most people found that hard to imagine. How could a person who's always in the limelight possibly be lonely? People tend to believe that someone like Marilyn Monroe would be deluged with invitations. But the fact was that because of her fame and glamour, people thought Marilyn Monroe was unapproachable. So instead of having many friends, she was a very lonely person.

This is why having someone to love and share your time with is part of my definition of happiness. Marilyn Monroe didn't, and she was consumed by her loneliness. I think many women, especially widows, can understand that. In my own situation, I had Mel to love and share with for fourteen years.

When he died, I suffered a deep loss. But I knew I could not allow myself to be consumed with self-pity. Instead, I put on a happy face as best I could and attended our scheduled meetings just four days later. I kept myself so busy I didn't have time to feel sorry for myself, because I knew self-pity was destructive. I believe that when you lose a loved one, you must know that he's now in a better place, and our grief is really grief for ourselves. Life is for the living, and we must carry on our daily lives.

We also have to remember that just because we are feeling sad, that doesn't mean other people are. As my first Christmas without Mel approached, I simply could not find the heart to put up a tree. Then it occurred to me that there would be nearly four hundred Directors in Qualification in my home the week before Christmas, and they would be expecting to see my home looking festive. I didn't want to rain on their parade, so I decided to put up a tree, because I knew they would be disappointed if I didn't.

I had the same battle with self-pity the month Mel died. He died on the seventh of July, and on the twenty-second I was scheduled to entertain the Directors in Qualification who were in Dallas, just as I have always done over the years. I did it, but it was the first time I'd done it without Mel. He'd always stood beside me to greet them at the door. He'd help serve the cookies and tea, and he'd always give an informal talk. I felt lost without him, but they never knew it, because I didn't let them know.

With Mel gone, there is an empty space in my heart. But I am fortunate in having so many wonderful people to love. So often I have the privilege of sharing with the women who work with our company. Not long ago, for example, I received a tear-stained letter from one of our Consultants in Atlanta. The letter began, "Dearest Mary Kay, I'm sitting at my kitchen window this morning watching my little girl run on two good legs. And it suddenly came to me that I owe this miracle to you." She went on to explain that her little daughter had been born with a deformed leg, and the family was unable to afford the many operations needed to correct the problem. Knowing how cruel children can be, the woman dreaded the thought of her child entering school with that handicap.

Then, when the little girl was about three, the woman attended a Beauty Show, and realized that *she* could do the same thing she had watched that Consultant do. So she became a Beauty Consultant, and for years she saved every single penny she made and put it into a fund for the operations for her little girl. When she wrote to me, the operations had been completed and the child now had two good legs! This was a woman who knew how to love and share with her family. And I'm so glad she shared with me, too. Just knowing that one child will lead a normal life is worth all the trials and tribulations of building this company.

The third part of my formula for happiness is always having something to look forward to. In my case, this ties in with the first two ingredients. I look forward to enjoying my work as much as I always have, and I look forward to being with people I love and can share with. I think it's vital to always have something "at the end of the rainbow." Once you approach your dream, it's important to find still another dream. Haven't you always found it to be true that anticipation is often more exciting than the actual realization of your goal? Children are more likely to enjoy anticipating their birthdays, for instance, more than the actual day itself. The same is true of a student anticipating summer vacation or graduation. In our business, we often see what a thrill anticipation can be. When a Director is working to win her first Cadillac, she and her whole unit are excited. But once she realizes her dream, the excitement wears off, and everyone goes about business as usual. I think most people have that same experience with their first house, first fur coat, first diamond ring, and just about any other "once-in-a-lifetime" thrill. Once the "dream" is realized, its object is no longer so important.

I think it's healthy to always have something to reach for,

and to find a new dream once an old dream is realized. By doing this, you stay enthusiastic and excited. I'm sure this accounts for the high energy level many people enjoy. I know that is what keeps me going strong.

Claude Bristol wrote a beautiful book, *The Magic of Believing,* and in that book he described his observations as a newspaper reporter. He saw people die while others just as sick got well; he watched football teams win while other teams just as good lost. As a result of studying all these men and women all over the world, he wrote his book, in which he says, "Gradually I discovered that there is a golden thread that makes life work, and that thread can be named in a single word—BELIEF!" Bristol saw in action the power of belief, and he recorded what he saw—people with BELIEF do FANTASTIC THINGS!

We all need a reason to get up in the morning. We need to keep doing new things we enjoy, and finding new excitements. My own dream is that Mary Kay Cosmetics will someday become the largest and best skin care company in the world. And this is not a starry-eyed dream, either—we're certainly on target so far.

The really happy person is one who never finds the end of the rainbow. I've enjoyed so many things during my lifetime—far more than I would ever have dreamed. I still find it difficult to wait for the sun to come up each morning, because every day there's something exciting in store. And every single day of my life, I thank God for giving me so much happiness.

⌒16⌒
You Can't Outgive God

The other day, I received an envelope with twenty $1 bills, along with a note from a Director asking me to autograph each bill and send them back to her to award to her Consultants. This happens frequently in Mary Kay, and I always write the same thing beside my name: "Matthew 25:14-30." That, of course, is the parable of the talents. I really believe that we are meant to use and increase whatever God has given us. The scripture tells us that when we do, we shall be given more. And that truth has been illustrated in my life dramatically, but once very specially, and I'd like to tell you about it.

A few years ago, the pastor of my church approached me one Sunday and asked me to address the congregation about raising funds for the children's building.

I have to admit that my first reaction was a sigh, well concealed, I hope. The fund raising for the children's building had been going very slowly. Each Sunday for some time, a member of the congregation had made a plea for the special collection, but the results were discouraging. At the rate of $600 to $1,000 a Sunday, we would not have that building for a long, long time. In recent months, the building committee had begun asking lay persons to address the congregation, thinking that might have a special effect. But the results were no different. No matter who spoke, we just couldn't top that

$1,000 a week. At that rate, we'd never see the building started.

With all this in mind, I felt a little hesitant about accepting the responsibility for a Sunday morning speech about the building fund. In addition, I hadn't been involved in the Sunday School here, so I said to the pastor, "But I don't have anything to do with the children's work in our church. Why not ask someone who works in that area?"

"You do believe children should be brought up in the church?"

"Well, of course I do."

"Then say so."

He had me. "When?" I asked.

"How about six weeks from today?"

The pastor was wise. I'm sure he knew that people will agree to do anything that's six weeks away. Well, I thought, I can't do much worse than anyone else has done. I may as well give it a try.

"I'll do it," I said.

The six weeks seemed to go by quickly because I was very busy at the office and had some traveling commitments as well. But in the back of my mind, I was searching for the right words for my plea to the congregation. It bothered me that I hadn't already written my speech, because I usually plan my schedule down to the minute.

Mel and I were in Chicago at a meeting the week before I was to give my speech, and I just didn't have time to sit down and write it. We arrived home well after midnight on the night before my Sunday speech. I was worried about it and I was still waiting for the right words. I convinced myself that it would be better to get a good night's sleep and plan my speech in the morning.

But Mel and I overslept. When I awoke and looked at the clock, it was after ten. I had less than an hour to get my thoughts in order and be at the church! It takes me longer than that to get dressed every morning. *When* was I going to write my speech? I had fully intended to have some quiet time this morning to work up the very best talk I could. And now. For about five seconds, I thought longingly of just staying home. But that was impossible. I had to keep my promise.

Mel was already racing around getting ready, and so was I. I grabbed the first dress I saw in my closet, and as I was slipping it on, I thought, "Lord, fill my mouth with worthwhile words, and stop me when I've said enough." Obviously the speech was going to be in His hands, for I didn't even have time to think this morning!

"You'll have to tell me what to say, Lord," I prayed. And then I stopped dead in the middle of putting on my makeup, because a thought had come to me so clearly and suddenly that I was shocked: "Mary Kay, tell the congregation you will match whatever they give today."

The thought was so vivid that I put down the makeup I was holding and said out loud, "Wait just a minute, Lord! I've got to think this over!" Fortunately, Mel didn't hear me talking away in my dressing room, and I didn't say anything to him. "He'll think I'm crazy!" I thought. If I even implied that God had spoken to me, anybody would be entitled to suggest that I needed a little more rest than I'd been getting. Talking to God is one thing. Many people do that. And, of course, some people say that God has spoken to them. But I'd never personally known anyone who said that. And I had never had God speak back to me—this was the closest I'd ever come.

In the car, I had a moment to think and pray, and I was tempted to tell Mel about the idea. "Don't you dare," I said to myself, so we rode in silence. I tried to gather my thoughts for my little speech; but all I could think about was that sentence that had come into my head so very clearly and so unexpectedly: "Mary Kay, tell the congregation you will match whatever they give today."

By the time we got to church, the choir was in place and the service was about to begin. We had to tiptoe down the side aisle to reach our seats. We'd hardly sat down when the pastor called me up to the pulpit.

As I walked up, I realized that I still had no idea at all

what I was going to say. Once again I said silently, "This is in Your hands, Lord." Then I found myself talking about my years of teaching Sunday School in my Houston church. I had worked there with the beginners, four- and five-year-old children, and I had really seen the value of teaching them the Bible at an early age. I talked about how important it is to teach children the difference between right and wrong. And I remember quoting Proverbs, "Train up a child in the way he should go, and when he is old, he will not depart from it."

Then I heard myself saying, "You know, we've all been talking about this building for quite some time. And we've been getting six hundred dollars, and maybe on great weeks, a thousand dollars, each Sunday. At this rate, these children are going to have grandchildren before the building is built. We must do something about this."

"You've heard me talk about our company and how we operate on a cash basis. Well, the Mary Kay Foundation will match whatever you give today."

Silence. I took a deep breath and went on.

"You know, we operate on a no-credit basis, so I don't want pledges from you today—I want cash or checks! Whatever you give today, the Mary Kay Foundation will match."

There, I had done it. I glanced at Mel. Since I had not talked to him about this, and since he was retired and might not be able to afford this offer, I really couldn't do it in both our names. I didn't want to do it in just my name, either, because I thought it might hurt his feelings. So I had made the offer in the name of our foundation, even though I knew those funds were already committed and additional funds weren't available for this purpose. Whatever the amount was, I knew I was going to have to match it *personally!*

Mel looked shocked, and so did a few other people. But for the most part, the congregation just sat there, and I really couldn't see any reaction at all. As I walked back to my seat, I was already berating myself for a speech that had totally failed. "Gee, you're really great," I thought. "You can sell cosmetics, but you can't sell God's work."

*Mary Kay
Sales Directors*

Dalene White

Cynthia Coupe

Anne Thompson

Nancy Tietjen

Ruell Cone

Helen McVoy

Shirley Hutton

Mary McDowell

Mary Kay autographs pictures for winners in contest.

Receiving the Horatio Alger Award from Dr. Norman Vincent Peale, 1978

Unit Club members. Those in fur coats are Half a Million Dollar Club members.

*1981
Seminar*

With Evangeline Escalanto, Queen of Consultants, Court of Personal Sales

Mary Kay and Marie Aquinaldo, Queen of Consultants, Court of Recruiting

Mary Kay by pink Cadillac

With son Richard Rogers, Awards Night

When the pastor finished his sermon, he paused and then added, "I had some difficulty keeping your attention this morning. I hope it's because you were thinking about Mary Kay's offer." Then he looked over at me and said, "Mary Kay, I happen to know that a lot of our members make out their checks before they come to church. I'm sure many people don't have their checkbooks with them. Would it be all right if we gave them until five this afternoon?"

"That's fine," I said. Well, he seemed to think they might respond; I hoped he wasn't wrong.

When five o'clock came, I found myself close to the telephone waiting for it to ring. How much had been given? But nobody called. I kept checking my watch, and the hours kept passing. With each hour, I became more discouraged. Obviously, the collection was so small they were embarrassed to tell me about it. The later it got, the worse I felt. Usually I would talk about my worries to Mel, but I was just too embarrassed to talk about this. When we went to bed that night, I still hadn't heard a thing.

It was about ten the next morning when I finally received a call from the chairman of the building committee.

"I was waiting for you to call last night," I said. "What happened?"

"Well," he said, "we had a meeting about this after church last night and it was quite late."

"Oh. Was it that bad?"

"Oh, no, on the contrary. It was phenomenal."

Phenomenal? A thousand? I thought. Maybe more. Maybe two thousand! Or even five thousand?

"What do you mean?" I asked him.

"Well, Mary Kay," he said carefully, "now, before I tell you the figure, I want to tell you what we were debating at our meeting."

"Yes?"

"We spent some time talking about this, and we decided that we are not going to hold you to your offer. I have been charged with the responsibility of making that absolutely clear to you. We know you didn't expect this, and we didn't either."

"I made the offer," I said, "and I'll stick to it."

"Now, you don't have to, I want you to know that. We would certainly understand if you didn't."

"How much?" This was sounding more like $5,000, I thought, maybe $10,000. If so, how wonderful! He still hesitated. Maybe $20,000? I thought jubilantly.

Finally he spoke. "$107,748."

Well, I was the person who had gone to bed last night just praying they had at least collected a thousand dollars. I have never had such mixed feelings in my life. That $107,748, along with mine and what we already had, would be enough to start the building! I had asked God to tell me what to say, and He sure had. It had succeeded beyond my wildest dreams.

On the other hand, my pledge came back to me very clearly: they had to give cash—and so did I—today!

"Are you there?" he asked when there was silence on my end of the line.

"Yes." I sighed. My mind was working furiously. I don't leave that kind of cash in my passbook savings account. As money comes in, I invest it. But those other members came up with it, and I would, too, somehow. The only solution that occurred to me was to cancel my next appointment and set about arranging a loan from the bank.

"Now, you don't *have* to," he began again.

"I know, I know. And that's very considerate of you. But I certainly intend to match the collection. In fact, you be sure the building committee knows that it is definitely my pleasure."

I hope I sounded cordial, but I'm not sure, because the moment I hung that phone up I had my head in my hands. That was a lot of cash—about one hundred times more than I had expected to need. "Okay, Lord," I said, "you got me into this. Now you get me out. How am I going to get this money?" Then the phone rang. It was Richard.

Here I have to backtrack and explain something. A while

back, Richard had come to me with an investment proposal.

Richard had spent approximately one year investigating a seismic technique for finding oil that had been developed by a friend of his, a geologist.

He was very excited about this potential venture and had encouraged me to invest in two oil wells. I trusted his judgment and told him, "Go ahead." I personally invested in two wells and from that day to this, I had never given those wells a thought.

Richard was very excited that Monday morning when he called me, just minutes after my conversation with the chairman of the building committee. "I've never seen anything like it in my life!" he said. "Everything you put your hand to turns to gold."

"What do you mean?"

"Those oil wells," he said, "remember? I've just heard that they came in, not one, but *both* of them! And both *gushers*! It's unbelievable! Do you know what those wells are worth?"

"Tell me." I'm sure I'd stopped breathing. I just had a funny feeling.

"Between the two of them," he said, "your share will be more than a hundred thousand dollars this month."

I can assure you, it was a very humble and grateful woman who took that contribution to the church at noon that day. The money I borrowed from the bank would be paid off by the end of the month with the revenues from the oil wells!

It reminded me of something I learned in Sunday School as a little girl—in a classroom, incidentally, not nearly so nice as those in our new children's building. They taught us that you never need to be afraid of giving for God—because he will always see to it that you get back a hundredfold. That's what the parable of the talents is all about. The more you give, the more you get. You can't outgive God.

～17～
Think Pink

I have gained a "pink reputation" over the years since 1963, so what I'm about to say may come as a surprise to a lot of people: *pink is not necessarily my favorite color!* I don't really prefer any one color, but I would have to say, if put to the test, that yellows and blues are equally pleasing to me. It is true, however, that in the world of Mary Kay Cosmetics, we do "think pink." From a business point of view, there's a reason for that.

When the company was begun in 1963, almost every home had a white bathroom. I also noticed that people had all kinds of deodorants, hair sprays, and cosmetics on the counters in their bathrooms. Things haven't changed much over the years. When I was looking for houses recently, I couldn't help noticing that it was still true. The beautiful marble and gold bathrooms in the most expensive houses in Dallas were littered with these ugly, garish containers.

Since people do leave their toiletries out, I wanted to package our cosmetics so beautifully that women would *want* to leave them out. So I was looking for a color that would make a beautiful display in all those white bathrooms. There were some shades of blue that were attractive, but the prettiest complementary color seemed to be a delicate pink. It also occurred to me that pink is considered a more feminine color. But my main reason for choosing it was that delicate pink seemed to look prettier than anything else in those white tile bathrooms. And from that, I gained a *pink* reputation!

Today, many people throughout the nation associate Mary Kay Cosmetics with pink Cadillacs. And there's no question that people do take notice when a pink Cadillac pulls up to an intersection. The color has everything to do with it. Occasionally I used to drive Mel's Lincoln Continental, and although it was a beautiful automobile, it just didn't get the attention a pink Cadillac attracts. When I drive mine, everyone notices and somehow I receive special courtesy from other drivers. (Directors who drive pink cars have also noticed this.) If I'm waiting at an intersection to pull into traffic, I'm always allowed to go through! The pink Cadillac has become such a hit that it is the core of our awards program. In fact, we give General Motors such a large order every year that they now call our color "Mary Kay Pink."

I'm sure the pink Cadillacs have done the most to build our pink reputation, which seems now to be very firmly established. In fact, many people are surprised when they visit our international headquarters in Dallas to find that the building isn't pink! At least, they expect the *inside* to be pink, and they often ask me why the windows are gold instead of pink. As for my office, they're absolutely amazed to discover that it isn't pink either, but a neutral beige. I do, however, have pink accents, such as throw pillows, pink cushions on the chairs, and pink flowers in the border of my beige carpeting. In case you're wondering, my home isn't pink either, with the exception of the bathroom. The bathroom walls, naturally, are pink to complement our cosmetics.

I have never had a pink office. My first two offices were done in lavender and purple, and my third one in blue. The lavender was just a preference, but I had a reason for the blue. In those days, whenever there was a recruiting problem or someone was unhappy, it was my responsibility to find a solution. Since we didn't have the staff then to handle such problems, the people came to my office. The office had light blue carpeting and walls, and it really seemed to be true that the blue had a tranquil effect.

When I chose pink for our packaging, I did not know of any psychological effect the color might have. It's very interesting to me that recent studies by psychologists in Los Angeles indicate that the color pink helps calm down overexcited or violent people. They have found that when unruly prisoners are put into pink cells, most become quiet within minutes. Apparently the color has a tranquilizing effect. Nobody was more surprised than I was to learn that pink had this quality.

One of our many Mary Kay traditions has to do with my pink bathroom. I'm not at all sure how it began, but it has become a tradition for the Directors in Qualification who come to Dallas each month for their week of training. I always invite them to a tea held in my home. My house is round, and in the bathroom I have a huge round sunken marble tub. Somehow it has become a must for every Director in Qualification to have her picture taken in that tub (clothed and without water in the tub, of course). This picture really is important to them. Once I received a letter from a girl who didn't make it through her qualification to become a Director. In the letter, she said, "I just know it's because I didn't have my picture taken in your bathtub!" Whether that's true or not, the bathtub tradition is firmly fixed.

As my reputation for liking pink grows, so does the number of pink gifts I receive. It seems as though anytime a Consultant or Director sees anything pink, she's reminded of me. So I receive pink presents almost all the time, things you wouldn't even imagine would be made in pink!

Manufacturers think of us, too. If a manufacturer makes anything he thinks we might purchase in volume, for an award, perhaps, he sends one in pink! Sometimes they're very clever. Once, for instance, we used a pink calculator as an award in a contest. Just the other day, I received, of all things, a little pink trampoline for indoor exercising! In addition to packaging our merchandise in pink, we equip our Consultants with pink beauty cases, pink pencils, etc. I also have stationery in a delicate pink with "Mary Kay" in gold across it.

As you can see, I do think pink, and we've given away pink things ranging from calculators to Cadillacs. But, while pink is beautiful, there are other colors I also like very much. And some things just don't seem at their best in pink. We have yet to give anybody a pink bumblebee or a pink mink!

~18~

Applause, Applause

I have never met a person who didn't enjoy being praised. I heard someone say that a woman could live a month on a sincere compliment—and all I can say to that is that it's a good thing she can! How many do you get? A housewife generally receives no recognition whatever for all the work she does. Most men just don't realize how difficult and time-consuming caring for a home can be. A woman could spend twenty-four hours a day on her house and never finish—and all of this without praise. The only time anybody ever notices housework is when you *don't* do it. Let's face it, housework is a thankless and endless job!

Now, most men receive a certain amount of recognition in their jobs. But the typical woman craves praise and needs it for her self-confidence. The only women who seem to receive any applause are beauty queens and movie stars. The fact is that most other women haven't been applauded since they graduated from high school! Women *need* recognition for their achievements. It gives them confidence.

It's very common for a prospective recruit to say, "Oh, I could never sell." What she's really saying is, "I don't have enough self-confidence." A lot of women have joined Mary Kay Cosmetics who didn't have enough confidence to order a pizza over the telephone. I don't think they could even have led in silent prayer! But we encourage them by praising even the smallest achievement. We applaud each little success one after another—and the first thing you know, they actually become successful. *We praise them to success!*

One Consultant who came for Director Training Week was so shy she couldn't even say, "Good morning." When I came in and said, "Good morning" to the group, she just tucked her head. She sat in the back row, painfully shy. Later, I learned that the reason she had joined the company was that she wanted to be able to stand in front of a group of six people and say, "My name is Rubye Lee" without fainting. She was that shy.

One of the staff members asked me what I thought about her, and I replied, "You know, I don't think that girl is going to make it. I've never met anyone *so* shy." Little did I know that one year later that same girl would be standing on stage at Seminar holding thousands of people in the palm of her hand! She delivered a speech so powerful she received a standing ovation. She's absolutely tremendous, and today has risen to National Sales Director. All she needed all along was someone to bolster her confidence!

Let me give you another example of "praising people to success." It happened many years ago, when we were still at 1220 Majesty Drive. I was in my office one morning, and since our quarters were rather small, with just two offices and a sales meeting room, I couldn't help overhearing Helen McVoy outside my door talking to a Consultant.

"You had a thirty-five-dollar Show?" she exclaimed. "That's wonderful!"

Well, even in those days a thirty-five-dollar Show wasn't wonderful. I couldn't imagine who she was talking to, and why she might have said such a thing. So I opened my door to peek out, and Helen saw me.

"Oh, Mary Kay," she said, "may I present my new recruit? Last night, she had a thirty-five-dollar Show!" Helen paused for a moment and then added softly, "The first two

Shows she didn't sell anything—but last night . . . !"

Without that praise and encouragement, it's entirely possible that that new Consultant might never have held her fourth Show! Helen was praising her to success. Underlining a woman's confidence by praising each small success has enabled many women to achieve more than they ever thought was possible. It was John D. Rockefeller who said, "I will pay more for the ability to deal with people—than for any other commodity under the sun—sugar or wheat or flour!" I'm sure that this innate ability of Helen McVoy's to work with people is the reason she has become the highest-paid person in our company—earning more than $240,000 in commissions as a National Sales Director in 1980!!

Everyone loves to be admired. One of the most important lessons I ever learned was to pretend that every single person we meet has a sign around his or her neck that reads, "Make Me Feel Important." Absolutely everyone reponds to praise. I believe that if you had your choice of two gifts for your child, with one million dollars on one side of the scale and the ability to teach your child to think positively on the other, that the greater gift would be the gift of confidence. And you give that by praising.

Young people need to be recognized for their achievements, too. My grandson, Rick, recently played in a national championship soccer tournament in Miami, and he was so excited. Knowing how proud he is, when I see him I say, "How's my champion soccer player?" As you can imagine, he just beams. Those eleven-year-old soccer players *won* that tournament, too!

I heard a cute little story that illustrates how much praise matters to young people. It seems a mother and her teen-age daughter were having a discussion about the girl's boyfriend. "What does he like about you?" the mother asked.

"Oh, he thinks I'm beautiful and sweet and have a wonderful personality."

"That's nice. And what do you like about him?"

"The fact that he thinks I'm beautiful and sweet and have a wonderful personality!"

But I think when it comes to needing applause, grownups aren't that different from children. Did you ever notice how college football players get a star for their helmets every time they make a key play? Well, I don't suppose that's really much different from the gold stars children get at school for good performance. Everybody responds to praise, from a little child to a great big 250-pound macho linebacker! Praise certainly did a great deal for me when I was a little girl. My mother praised me for everything I did, and I grew to like that recognition and to want more of it. I liked being praised for selling the most tickets and receiving an award for being the best typist in my class. I enjoyed being in the limelight on the debating team. And I loved being applauded at extemporaneous speaking contests.

I've already talked about how much I wanted to win the Miss Dallas contest that Stanley Home Products held. Why did I work so hard? It certainly wasn't for the prize, a ribbon with "Miss Dallas" on it. I worked for the recognition. Since then, I've seen many other women work harder for a ribbon than they would have for an expensive gift or a cash prize. They may already have a Cuisinart, or whatever the prize may be. It's the recognition that they need. The desire for recognition is a powerful motivator. If you give somebody a forty-cent item in a $1 box with $100 worth of recognition, that's a thousand times more effective than giving a $100 item in the same box with forty cents worth of recognition!

We've found that housewives who are getting into the job market for the first time thrive on the praise we give them. No housewife *ever* has anyone in her family exclaim, "Oh, what a beautiful, clean floor!" "What nice, clean diapers! Aren't they white and fluffy!" (No matter what the television commercials say!) So often women who do volunteer work are not recognized for that, either. Many of our best people have been professional volunteers. When they come to us, they suddenly learn how much fun it is to receive recognition—and money—for their work. We find that very often it isn't the money that motivates a woman.

I think most women are willing to work hard for even a little bit of recognition. That's why we award a ribbon for a Consultant's first $100 Show, and another ribbon for her first $200 Show, and so on. That recognition is important to new Consultants. Recently a Director wrote to tell me that some of her people had won every single sales ribbon we have. "Where do I go from here?" she asked. I wrote back telling her to start praising those women toward recruiting, and then help them get on the road toward becoming Directors. Our Directors understand the importance of recognition. Many of them, for instance, give a Consultant a little costume jewelry bee for each person she recruits. By the time a Consultant comes to Dallas for DIQ week, it's not uncommon for her to have fifteen or twenty little gold-colored bumblebees on her jacket. By giving her those, her Director is giving her a visible sign of her achievement. "Look at her—she's an achiever!" those silent bumblebees say.

As important as recognition is, prizes are important, too, as symbols of recognition. I'll never forget one of the first sales contests I won. I worked very hard to win the top sales award, and would you believe, they gave me *a flounder light?* I didn't even know what it *was.* I found out later that it's something you use when you put on those long hip boots and wade out into the water and gig fish! I was proud of winning—but I can't imagine anything I wanted less.

I kept that flounder light around for years to remind me that if *I* ever got into the position of giving awards, I must never give a woman a flounder light! I'd try instead to choose prizes a woman would love to have. I thought the best prizes were things a woman wouldn't buy for herself, and we eliminated practical gifts. A woman will always think about her family before she considers herself. If you put a washing machine on one side of a scale and a mink coat on the other side, women are usually so practical that the washing machine wins. So that's why we give prizes like mink coats, pink Cadillacs, and diamonds.

We award countless diamond rings. Many women, I think, have never received a diamond except for an engagement ring, and they love them. When a woman is a star performer, it's just a matter of a few years before she has a diamond ring on every finger. I don't have to tell you how glad I was when it became fashionable to wear rings on each finger of both hands!

As I mentioned earlier, the diamond bumblebee has become the symbol of ultimate recognition at Mary Kay. The bumblebee's impressive "against all odds" aerodynamics made it the perfect symbol for women of accomplishment. So I decided to award a diamond bumblebee at Seminar to the Queens in the various awards categories. These Queens also receive such prizes as mink coats, Queen's rings, and pink Cadillacs—all things they certainly wouldn't buy for themselves. But the diamond bumblebee is the "crown jewel" among our people. Whenever you see someone in our organization wearing a diamond bumblebee, you know that she has been a Queen. It's the number-one status symbol.

Another status symbol our people wear is the red jacket. A Consultant is allowed to wear the red jacket when she has recruited three people. When she has five recruits and becomes a Team Leader, she receives an emblem for the pocket and special buttons that say, "TLC." That stands for Team Leader Consultant, but it also means Tender, Loving Care, because that's what a good Team Leader gives her recruits. When she has eight recruits, she gets a very striking new emblem for the pocket, and the old emblem comes off. Now she's a Future Director. We see many of these jackets at DIQ week and during Seminar. And, of course, they're often studded with tiny, gold-colored bumblebees, indicative of the number of recruits they have.

Women who reach the Sales Director level wear beautiful

designer suits. This year's suit, for example, is terra cotta, and a Director will have one of three blouses with it. The delicate pink blouse indicates you're a Director. The ivory blouse means you're a Senior Director, who has had one to four Directors come from her unit. The teal blouse is for Future Nationals, who have had five or more Directors from their units. Then for National Sales Directors, we have Ultrasuede suits, sometimes adorned with fur and very beautiful.

Outsiders are sometimes skeptical of all the awards and symbols we have at Mary Kay: "Aren't those women foolish," they'll say, "working so hard just for recognition?" But we're really not doing anything men haven't been doing since the beginning of civilization. Just look at the special uniforms, ribbons, stripes, and medals that the military uses to symbolize status. Men have risked their lives on the battlefields for the recognition of a medal and a cause they believed in.

We also recognize our outstanding people in our monthly magazine, *Applause!* People love to see their names in print, so we list our star salespersons for the previous month. We also include the names of top recruiters and DIQs who come to Dallas for training. Every issue is full of photographs: new Directors, DIQs, and Miss Go-Give of the month. Of course, we have noticed one thing about *Applause!*—when your name isn't in it, it isn't any good!

Each of our Sales Directors also sends out a monthly newsletter so that she can praise the members of her unit. In many cases, this means recognizing people who didn't make the news in *Applause!* For the Directors, we have a weekly company publication called *Director's Memo.* In the *Memo,* we often quote especially good things from Directors' newsletters. As I read their newsletters, I clip anything that's new or original or especially inspiring. We now have more than three thousand Directors' newsletters, and everybody aspires to be quoted in the *Director's Memo.* Again, it's a form of recognition.

I believe that public recognition is the finest form of praise. Newsletters are one very effective way of giving public recognition. Another way is the weekly sales meeting. All of our Directors hold these meetings, and they offer an excellent platform to praise individuals for their achievements. Being praised by a Director in front of peers is more gratifying than being praised in private. The enthusiastic applause and the presentation of ribbons and other awards adds an aura of excitement. This sort of recognition does wonders for a woman's self-esteem.

Giving praise where it is due is part of our philosophy in everything we do in Mary Kay. The praise begins at the first Beauty Show a woman attends, when we tell her how she looks after her facial. Then, when she expresses an interest in becoming a Consultant, we encourage her by telling her she can do it. Perhaps the time she needs praise most is after she has given her first Show. Even though the Consultant may have made some drastic mistakes, a wise recruiter will avoid criticism. Especially in the beginning, the Consultant needs praise for everything she did *right!*

I don't think people anywhere respond positively to criticism. Suppose a woman goes out and buys a new dress, and comes home and tries it on for her husband. If he says, "For goodness' sake, where did you get that—Goodwill?" he just blew $100, because chances are she'll never wear it again. I find that if you must criticize, it's best to sandwich it between two thick layers of praise, and just barely mention the criticism. For instance, when a Director goes to a Consultant's Show, she'll take two pages of notes. On one page, she writes down all of the good things the Consultant did. On the other, she lists all the problems. Invariably, after the Show the first thing the Consultant says is, "Tell me what I did wrong." They *all* say that. But instead, the Director says, "Let's talk about what you did right." And she encourages the Consultant by praising her strong points. When she does give criticism, she very carefully sandwiches it in between all the praise.

I think it's very important to be sure you are sincere when you give praise. Insincerity has a tendency to backfire.

I'll never forget the time that happened to me, when I was working for Stanley.

I always made a practice of complimenting my hostess on something I really liked about her house when I arrived. But at this particular party, I was very rushed. It was early December, our busiest season, and I was giving three parties a day. When I got to this house, I just didn't see a thing I could sincerely compliment. So as I was setting up, on the wall behind my table I noticed a painting of a hummingbird on an orchid, and I said, "What a *beautiful* painting!"

She said, "Oh, I'm so glad you like it. I painted it."

I couldn't think of anything else to say, so I complimented her again on it. It was obvious I left the impression that I really liked that painting.

Two weeks later, I went back to make her delivery. It was almost Christmas Eve, and I needed that money desperately for my children's Christmas presents. The woman gave me a warm welcome, and then she said, "You know, Mary Kay, I've been thinking about how much you liked my painting. And I'm going to give it to you for my order." Of course, there was nothing I could do but thank her. And I don't have to tell you what kind of Christmas we had that year. But I learned an invaluable lesson: *never* give insincere praise.

Giving praise is an integral part of our business. Our Consultants learn to praise the people they work with. Soon, giving praise becomes second nature. A Consultant begins to praise her husband and children. She applauds her family and lets them know how wonderful she thinks they are. And her habit of praising other people has a ripple effect, and enriches the lives of everyone she knows.

It was Emerson who said, "The only gift is a portion of thyself." And we give of ourselves when we give encouragement and honest praise. In the long run, we are the ones who gain, for it is true that all we send into the lives of others does come back into our own.

⌒ *19* ⌒

The Personal Touch

Many years ago, I stood in line for three hours so I could shake hands with the vice-president of sales of the company I worked for. We had never met, and to me it was a very special occasion. When I finally inched my way up to actually meet him, he did take my hand and say hello—but all the while he was looking over my shoulder to see how many people were behind me. He never even knew I was there. Even today, I hurt at the memory of that. Then and there I decided, "If I ever get to be the one they're shaking hands with, I'm going to put all my attention on the person in front of me—even if it means I never finish the line!"

As things turned out, people have stood in lines that long to shake my hand, and I have always tried my best to make every single person feel important. People have asked me, "How do you do it? Aren't you exhausted?" Of course, but I do it because I know how it feels to be brushed off by somebody who's important to you. And whether you're standing in a reception line or talking to your child after school, it's always important to focus all your attention on the person in front of you. If you can love that person, that's all the better. But you must never treat anyone in a way you wouldn't like to be treated yourself.

It's just amazing how important some personal attention

can be to people. It makes a bigger difference than you might think. For example, let me tell you about the time I went out to buy a car many years ago. They had just come out with the two-toned cars, and I had my heart set on a black-and-white Ford. I had waited to buy one until I saved up the purchase price, since it's always been my policy not to buy what I can't afford. It was my birthday, and I planned to give myself that beautiful car as a very special present. So, with the money in my purse, I walked into the dealer's showroom.

The salesman had apparently seen me getting out of my old, beat-up car, and figured I couldn't afford a new car. In any case, he didn't give me the time of day. He completely ignored me.

Well, I was determined to buy that car, so I asked to speak to the manager. He was out to lunch, and wouldn't be back until one. I didn't want to wait around the showroom for an hour with that rude salesman. So I went out to take a walk.

Just across the street, there was a Mercury dealer, and I decided I might as well look around his showroom since I had some time to kill. There was a yellow Mercury on the floor, and it cost quite a bit more than the Ford. The salesman there was very courteous and interested in me, and soon found out that it was my birthday. He excused himself for a minute, and when he came back we talked for a while. The next thing you knew, he was wishing me a happy birthday and placing a dozen red roses in my arms!

And that's how I came to buy a yellow Mercury instead of a black-and-white Ford!

I've always believed in the importance of the personal touch. For instance, every month when the DIQ class comes to Dallas, I invite them to tea at my home. I've done this for so long that it's become a tradition. Of course, as the classes have grown larger, it's been suggested that I rent a reception hall instead. After all, it is difficult to accommodate several hundred women in a private home. But I love having the DIQs as my guests. I serve them spiced tea and homemade cookies (I mix up batches of cookie dough and my housekeeper bakes and freezes them). The DIQs just love the idea that they're eating cookies that I made myself. They seem to like the cookies, too. In fact, we had so many requests for the recipes that my assistant, Jennifer, came up with the great idea of printing a DIQ Cookie Book, with twenty cookie recipes and the recipe for the spiced tea. Some of the DIQs take a cookie home with them for their children or a friend or a Consultant in their unit—because "it was made by Mary Kay." So it's obvious that my little personal touch matters to them.

The DIQs love to have their pictures taken with me, and so I do that, although this sometimes becomes somewhat overwhelming. I've often stood in front of my fireplace for hours while Polaroid photographs were taken of me with every single person there. It would go faster if I just passed them through quickly and didn't talk with anyone (and I've been advised to do that). But if I did, I think they would feel hurt. I know that this is important to them, so I always have something to say to each one.

To the DIQs, those photographs are important. At the Beauty Shows, the Consultants use a flip chart for their presentation that includes a picture of me, and they'll say, "And Mary Kay's the chairman of the board and a great-grandmother!" Half the time the women at the Show will yawn and say, "Oh, sure. That picture was probably taken when she was fourteen years old." But the DIQs then whip out the photograph we took in my house and say, "And last month this was taken of Mary Kay and me." All of a sudden there's interest and everyone wants to see it. The Consultants tell me this causes a lot of excitement, because the women can see the Consultant and how she looks at the moment, and there she is in the picture with me—so they know it's a current picture.

Now that our company has grown so large, the personal touch seems even more important, because people don't quite believe I'm a real person. Very often women will come up to me at Mary Kay functions and say, "I just can't believe it!

You're real! You're just like they said you were!" I think a personal word of encouragement is so important to these people. In almost every DIQ class, someone will say to me, "Mary Kay, do you remember when I met you at Jamboree and I was just a new Consultant, and you told me I'd be here someday?" Well, I have to confess that I can't remember everyone. But when I hear that, I know how much it means to people when I stop and say a few words to them at our various functions.

Every now and then, the personal touch makes a believer out of someone who thinks I'm more myth than reality. Recently, a man called long distance four times, and insisted on speaking to me. I was in a meeting, and Jennifer kept telling him I wasn't available, and offering to help. Finally, on the fourth call, he told her his reason for calling. "Look," he said, "my wife has become a Consultant and wants to place an order. But I'm not about to let her do it until I know what this company is all about. I want to speak to Mary Kay!"

When I got out of my meeting at seven, I found his name and a note from Jennifer on top of my phone calls. So I called him. "Well, I've already looked up your company," he began, "and I found out you're doing millions in sales. Actually, I'm amazed that you returned my call. I never really expected to hear from you."

It turned out that he also owned a business, although not as large as ours, and he was impressed by our personal touch. The last thing he said to me was, "Mary Kay, you made a believer out of me by returning my call." I was glad to hear that, because he had been giving his wife a bad time, and now he was obviously going to be more supportive of her career.

It's so important for our company to help Consultants win the support of their husbands. We write to the husband when a woman comes to Dallas for DIQ week. The letter explains to him how much she's learning and how beneficial this will be to her in the months to come. We mail the letter on the Monday the DIQ arrives, so her husband receives it just about the time the sink is full of dishes and he's getting a little uptight about having to do everything himself. I think these are important letters, and I sign each one personally.

As you might have guessed by now, we've been sending out Christmas cards, birthday cards, and anniversary cards to every single one of our people since we started this company. We send cards to more than 100,000 individuals, and we make certain that every birthday card is mailed on the right day. I personally design the cards. And, although I couldn't possibly sign that many cards every day, each card has a message in my handwriting, such as "A wonderful birthday to a wonderful person" or "Precious things are very few—that's why there must be just *one* of *you!*"

We also give an anniversary bracelet to each Consultant at the end of her first year with the company. It is a pretty gold-plated bracelet with a one-year charm. On each of her next three anniversaries, she receives another charm, and on the fifth, the charm has a diamond in it.

Each of our more than three thousand Directors also receives a Christmas and birthday gift. One year, for instance, we sent the Directors a "Ms. Bear" for Christmas. This was something Mel had given me for a Thursday gift. You pull its string and it says things like, "You're wonderful. You're headed for the top" or "I love you. You are terrific. You can do anything." Another year, I sent each Director a sonic jewelry cleaner.

I also demand that every letter addressed to me receive a reply. I feel that anyone who cared enough to write deserves an answer and as soon as possible, preferably mailed within twenty-four hours. Of course, as the volume of my mail has grown, it's become impossible for me to handle everything myself, so we have a system for answering letters that pertain to certain problems.

Erma Thomson, who became my personal assistant in our third year of business, is fantastic at helping me personalize our business. She just may be the best "people person" in the whole company. If a Consultant or a Director calls up distraught and wants to speak to me, Erma takes the call when I'm not available. Invariably she can soothe the person's feelings and get to the bottom of the problem. She's become the person the Directors all depend on when something has to be handled quickly. So often they'll call her and say, "Erma, can you do something about . . ."

Erma also knows exactly what arrangements have to be made to ensure that the little things get done, like seeing to it that there's a fresh rose from me in each DIQ's room when she arrives at her hotel. For one national meeting, Erma had cheese and crackers placed in each National Sales Director's room as a gift from me. They loved that, because they're all familiar with my story about my first Stanley convention, where I had nothing to eat for three days but cheese and crackers.

There are many things, of course, that I handle myself. One is sympathy cards. I send perhaps a dozen handwritten notes a day to those of our people who are seriously ill or who have just lost a loved one. I have had some little poems printed up that have been meaningful to me, and I always try to include one of those. People seem to be very touched by that personal note and poem. When I can, I also make surprise phone calls to extend my condolences or tell them to hurry up and get well, and that we love them. A call like that is such a little thing, but it always seems to do wonders in lifting a person's spirits.

We've worked hard at keeping a family atmosphere in our organization, regardless of our size. Nobody is addressed as Mr. or Mrs. or Ms. here. Richard is called Richard by everybody, and I'm called Mary Kay. If people call me Mrs. Ash, I think they either don't know me or they're unhappy with me. We don't have titles on the doors, either, and unless there's a conference going on, our office doors are open. As you can imagine, people will often walk right into your office and interrupt you if the door's open. But we feel it's important for everyone to know that they can do that when they need to talk to you. I don't know where else you could have the mail boy drop by the chairman's office and sit down and chat for a few minutes. But our young man does do that here. He visits with me on a regular basis, and tells me about his dreams and aspirations.

You don't find many closed doors in our company, and you also won't find executive bathrooms or executive dining rooms. We have a very pretty cafeteria. I've been told that it looks more like a country club than a company cafeteria, and it's not just for executives—it's for everyone.

As our company keeps getting larger, I'm sometimes embarrassed by meeting someone on an elevator that I don't know. If I can tell the person works for the company by the papers he or she is carrying, I'll say, "Hi, I don't think I've met you. I'm Mary Kay." Sometimes this flusters people because they haven't had a chance to get to know me. So we decided to try to help that situation by starting a new program. Several times a month, a group of perhaps twenty-five new employees comes into my office to meet with me. These are people who have just joined us, and they always come in very formal and straight faced. So I talk to them a little about the company, and tell a few anecdotes, and they relax and begin to smile. I think these meetings help them see me more as a friend than as the chairman of the board.

Occasionally we have had executives join us who couldn't adjust to our family atmosphere. This can happen when they've worked for another company with a more hierarchical system. One executive in particular not only kept his door closed, but refused to talk to visiting Consultants and Directors. At times, he was downright rude to them. That's just the way things were done in his former company; hard to believe, isn't it? Finally I had to say to him, "Look, the only reason you have your job is because of those Consultants and Directors. They're the most important people in the world as far as we're concerned. Don't you agree that you should feel that way about them, too?" He did see that his attitude was wrong, and now he puts out the red carpet when any Consultant or Director approaches him. He's much happier at his work now—and needless to say, so is everyone else.

Most executives who come to us from other companies aren't used to our family atmosphere—but when they adjust to our way, they love it. They like knowing that if they have a problem they can approach Richard or me. Any employee can. We do encourage employees to discuss their problems with their supervisors, because in most cases a problem can be resolved right there. But if it's a major crisis, they all know they can come in and talk to one of us.

Unfortunately, some companies don't treat their people very well at all. One man who worked for a firm here in Dallas had a very sad experience. His wife went into labor in the middle of the night, and when he took her to the hospital they found it was a breech birth, which can be a very difficult situation. For two days, there was a possibility she wasn't going to live. It was touch and go, and he stayed by her bedside and waited. With all that going on, he forgot to call his office—which was as it should have been. She was the only thing on his mind.

When he returned to work, he didn't have a job, because he hadn't called in. Even after he explained what had happened, they just said, "Well, if you don't think any more of your job than that, you're fired."

This man applied for a position with us because he had heard that we do value the family. He knew that we place the family above the company, and if the same thing had happened with one of our employees, we would have been proud of what he did. He's working for us now, and when he talks about what happened to him, he says, "Mary Kay would have sent pink flowers instead of a pink slip." That is our reputation, and I think it pays off. Today, we have a waiting list of people who want to work for us. And the morale of our employees is just wonderful!

In our company, everyone values the personal touch. We

believe in courtesy. Not too long ago, a man came in and sat down in our reception area without asking for anyone. Finally, the receptionist asked him, "Is there something I can do for you, sir?"

"Nothing," he replied. "I just came in here to recharge my batteries. I call on companies all day long, and so many people are so sarcastic and nasty, and they bark at me, 'What do you want?' But when I come here, everybody is so happy and smiling, it's like coming into the sunshine. It makes me feel good just to visit this company."

We've had out-of-towners tell us that when they ask to be taken to Mary Kay Cosmetics, their cabdrivers treat them like VIPs. "To Mary Kay Cosmetics, I sure will," the driver replies. "That's the nicest company in town. When I go there to pick up a passenger, they're the only ones who ask me to come in and sit down. They even offer me a cup of coffee when I have to wait on a fare. Other companies chase me out."

I believe in the personal touch that makes every human being feel appreciated. As somebody once said, "The oil of appreciation makes the wheels of progress turn." In our company, we do things that aren't normally done in the business world, but I believe that personal touch has helped to build this company.

Recently a man wrote to me, "Mary Kay, the company is growing so fast, I'm worried that there may soon be a day when that personal touch is gone."

I wrote back and explained to him that I worried about that when we had 1,000 people. Then I worried about it when we were 5,000; and 10,000; and 20,000; and I'm still worrying about it now, with over 100,000 people in our organization. I also told him that I'll *always* be concerned about the personal touch—and do everything in my power to see that we never lose it. Richard feels this way, too, and it gives me great comfort to know that, through him, this important philosophy will continue.

❧20❧

The Proof of the Pudding...

Mary Kay women come from every imaginable background and represent every religion; we attract young women, women in mid-life, and grandmothers. They live in large cities and rural ones across the United States, and in Canada, Guam, Puerto Rico, Australia, and Argentina. I wish I could tell you about every one of them, because each one has a very special story.

With all their differences, they share a common bond—a spirit of loving and giving which I believe is unique in the business world. When I began this company, I seemed to stand alone in my belief that a business could be predicated on the golden rule. Now, the Mary Kay family has shown that women can work and prosper in that spirit, while achieving great personal success.

For some of our women, success may mean earning enough money to send their children to college, or to buy larger homes. Others set far higher financial goals. However they may define success, Mary Kay women agree that their faith and their families come before their careers. They live the Mary Kay philosophy—God first, family second, job third.

Throughout this book, I have told you about many of the Consultants and Directors who have become successful—professionally and personally. I believe their stories illustrate the real success of Mary Kay Cosmetics. The most valuable assets of our company cannot be found on our balance sheets, for our most important assets are our people. No matter how much profit a company makes, if it doesn't enrich the lives of its people, that company has failed. Our true wealth is measured by the thousands of women who have found our company to be the way to attain richer, fuller lives. In my opinion, that's the *proof of the pudding...*

In this chapter, I will tell you about a handful of Mary Kay success stories, because I feel just like a proud mother who wants to show off her beautiful children. But as you know, a mother can show just so many pictures! My publisher has asked that I select just eight women out of more than 100,000—and believe me, this was not an easy task. After all, *I love all of my children.* There are so many deserving and very special people I would like to include; for example, the National Sales Directors in our company in 1980 who earned an *average* of more than $140,000.

So please keep in mind that these eight women have been chosen to represent many, many others. I will present each one to you individually. Then you will read their stories as they tell them, from the heart.

DALENE WHITE our very first Consultant, started with Mary Kay Cosmetics on our opening day. She was also our first Director and our first Senior Director. In January, 1971, Dalene and Helen McVoy shared the honor of becoming our first National Sales Directors, and later they became our first "Mary Kay Millionaires." By early 1979, Dalene's total Mary Kay earnings had surpassed the million-dollar mark. She has earned so many Mary Kay firsts that there is just not room to list them all. Dalene's annual earnings for 1980 were $200,255. A Fort Worth resident, she tutored dyslexic students before she joined our company.

When Mary Kay's husband died just one month before the company's grand opening, I agreed to help out for a little while. I enjoyed teaching, riding in rodeos, and singing with the Fort Worth Opera, and when I picked up that blue beauty case (yes, the first beauty case was blue—not pink!) to book the first Mary Kay Beauty Show, I had no intention of making a career out of it. In fact, I had never even worn cosmetics until then!

I had been a business associate of Mary Kay's husband, and when I started with the company I really didn't know her that well. But you don't have to be around her very long to realize how dynamic she is. Very early, I saw that this company was unique. At the time, there just weren't many really good opportunities for women in sales, and Mary Kay Cosmetics was designed especially to provide an opportunity for women to achieve all the success they wanted. Mary Kay's genius for sales creativity and dealing with people was obvious even in the handwritten notes she gave me for my first formal sales presentation. She had a wonderful ability to make people believe in themselves. And her sincerity shone through her encouragement.

She's also the world's greatest motivator. I remember how proud I was when I finally came in with a $400 week. Mary Kay told me how well I had done, and then she added, "And next week, Dalene, you'll do even better!" Well, I went out there and broke my neck so I wouldn't let her down, and I did do better the next week.

But my strongest reason for becoming a full-time Consultant, and then reaching for other goals, was that I believed absolutely in Mary Kay. I had no doubt at all that she would lead the company to greatness. You could feel a special quality in the air whenever you were in the same room with her. I knew she was a WINNER!

Perhaps having developed a beautiful friendship with Mary Kay has been the most precious thing about this business to me. One reason I identify closely with her is that our philosophies are so similar. I had never verbalized my priorities be-

fore I met Mary Kay, but they were the same as hers—God first, family second, career third.

Of course, I've had great financial rewards for my work in this company. I grew up on a two-thousand-acre ranch in Leakey, Texas, and I've been able to buy some five hundred acres of my own on one side of Dad's ranch, and an additional sixty acres on the other side. There was a time when buying that kind of land was only a dream, but now my dreams have come true.

At the last Seminar, as I stood onstage looking out at those eight thousand happy, enthusiastic people, tears began to run down my cheeks. I just couldn't help it. I thought about how far we had come since that first day, just seventeen years ago, when there were only nine of us. And I thought about how many women have become successful and self-confident because of this company.

Obviously, a day will eventually come when Mary Kay is no longer with us. And we'll say to everyone, "Now, this is what Mary Kay would tell us" and "Mary Kay would want us to do this." Even now, when one of my girls has a problem, I'll say, "What do you think Mary Kay would do in your situation?" You know, it's very important for each of us to perpetuate everything Mary Kay stands for—and we will!

Even though the company began as the dream of one woman, today thousands of women all over the world share in that dream. They represent Mary Kay's philosophies of integrity and honesty. And those principles are timeless. In the years to come, we have only to refer to these principles and we'll be carrying out the Mary Kay way of business—and the Mary Kay way of life.

CYNTHIA COUPE, a resident of MacGregor, Queensland, and a former registered nurse, joined the company in April, 1971, just two months after Mary Kay Cosmetics opened in Australia. In June, 1973, Cynthia qualified as a Director. She holds a record for being the Top Unit Director in Australia for four consecutive years. Her highest monthly commission check to date was in excess of $4,000.

Before I joined Mary Kay, I ran my own nursing service with a staff of ninety nurses. I have always put family before career. That's why I started a program where nurses could work part time and be with their families when they needed to be. Everybody said the service would fail, but it worked out very well.

One night, I called a nurse who told me she couldn't go to work until eleven, because she was doing a Beauty Show. When I asked her if she would put cosmetics before nursing, she replied, "Every time."

Well, that made me curious enough to have a facial, and immediately I bought the Basic from her and signed the agreement. For the next two and a half months, I worked for Mary Kay part time, and I loved it so much that I decided to sell my business to do this full time. Would you believe that by my second full-time week I was making more money as a Mary Kay Consultant than I had previously made as a nurse? And I had been in nursing for many, many years!

Although we're quite a distance from the States, our orders are delivered within just seven days. You see, the raw products are shipped here and then manufactured in Melbourne, near our Australian headquarters. We do just about everything exactly like our American sisters. We use the same sales materials, and we follow Mary Kay's beautiful philosophies to the letter. I even get up at five every morning just like Mary Kay—but I've been doing that all my life. Mary Kay has given us a map, and it leads us to accomplishment and fulfillment. All you have to do is follow it.

We receive pink cars for prizes, too. I drive a pink Holden, a GM car made in Australia, which is our equivalent to a Cadillac. After the 60 Minutes program which featured Mary Kay was shown in Australia, there was quite a lot of interest, and people began to recognize our pink cars. I kept finding notes on my windshield that said, "I've been looking every-where for Mary Kay products. Would you please call me?"

There are some differences in doing business here. Austra-lian women are not yet as liberated as American women, so it's somewhat more difficult to recruit. And I believe women down here have less positive self-images than American women. Then, too, we don't tend to be as cosmetic-oriented. We're just beginning to learn that it's unhealthy to go out in the sun and bake your skin. So the Mary Kay training in skin care is really needed here.

I've been to six Seminars in Dallas, and even though it's an expensive trip, it's worth every penny to me. It's really exciting to see eight thousand Mary Kay Consultants and Di-rectors in the Dallas Convention Center. The American Semi-nar is on such a large scale compared to ours! The American Directors' meetings are as large as the entire Mary Kay sales force in Australia. It really opens my eyes as to what can be done in this business. And I'm planning on being the first Na-tional Sales Director in Australia!

ANNE THOMPSON, now a Bostonian, was born and raised in Dallas. Anne spent much of her time working as a volun-teer fund raiser for the Junior Symphony Society and the Dal-las Ballet before she joined the company in July, 1969. In 1974, Anne received the Miss Go-Give Award, and in August, 1976, she became a National Sales Director. More than any other individual, Anne has been responsible for helping our com-pany grow in Canada. Her annual earnings in 1980 were $145,689.

When my husband and I lived in Dallas, I was active with the symphony and the ballet, and after we moved to Richmond, Virginia, I became involved in Junior League-type activities. I'd really only known fund raising and had never worked for pay.

Then in the summer of '69 while I was visiting home, my

cousin, who is a very successful real estate developer, said to me, "Anne, you spend all your time raising money for some-body else—have you ever thought about making some money for yourself?" He suggested I look into Mary Kay Cosmetics. That was the first time I had ever heard of the company.

My cousin suggested I call (National Sales Director) Carolyn Savage to learn more, so I telephoned her and asked her to mail some information to me. She said that wouldn't be fair, and suggested we have lunch together. I had to fly back to Richmond the next day, but I reluctantly accepted.

That lunch turned out to be a five-hour conversation; I was mesmerized by what Carolyn had to say. She's quite an elegant woman, and I was impressed by her pink Cadillac, all her jewelry, and her confidence. She just oozed success.

My daddy was a partner in one of the largest pipeline construction companies in the country, and I have a great deal of respect for his business judgment. So I sat down with him to get his opinion on his "little girl" selling Mary Kay Cosmetics. If he had said no, I wouldn't have joined the company. But he said, "Honey, I don't see any reason why you shouldn't give it a try." Well, since Carolyn had recommended that I buy enough merchandise to keep some inventory "in the store," I told my daddy that he was going to have to make me a little loan of $350. He gladly gave me a check. The next morning, Carolyn gave me a facial, and I went back to Richmond with my beauty case, a Consultant's Guide, and a lot of desire. That was the total extent of my initial training.

I have to admit I had some reservations. I couldn't help wondering how my Junior League sisters and fellow board members would react. I could just hear them whispering, "Can you imagine Anne Thompson selling cosmetics?" But that was my own hang-up, and something I had to get out of my system.

I'd done only a few Beauty Shows when my husband was offered a position as a newspaper editor in Boston. We made the move, and I quickly got involved with social work in Boston. *I wasn't spending much time with my Mary Kay career until one day a friend told me her husband had just given her a trip to Elizabeth Arden's as a birthday gift. I told her I wanted to give her a facial, because I could do the same thing for her for free! So she and a friend came over for facials, and both bought the Basic. That's how I began my Mary Kay career in Boston. Not long after that, Carolyn Savage telephoned and talked to me about the great potential the business had in New England. She agreed to come up and help me recruit, and that's when my business started to take off.*

I have to admit that when I came to Dallas for Director Training I had misgivings, especially about the singing they did, but by the fifth day I was so excited about the company that I could have flown back to Boston without a plane! My only worry was whether my New Englanders would accept the songs at our meetings. Again, that was just my hang-up. When I started to sing in front of my girls, they joined in and sang along.

As our unit production grew, we would sit around my dining room table and talk about our plans to develop all of New England. I can still see our husbands shaking their heads and saying, "Those poor things! I hope they're not too disappointed." We aren't disappointed. Today, we have several thousand Mary Kay people in this area, and we've expanded into Canada.

It was very natural for me to become active in developing Canada. I knew a lot of Bostonians who had been born in Canada, and they had relatives and friends across the border who were also eager to sell Mary Kay. After I became a National, I made a decision to help with the development of Canada. Canadians are such wonderful people! For three years, I spent two to two and a half weeks every month in Canada; I worked every province at least three times. One week, Mary Kay and I did a crisscross tour of Canada, so I was able to spend seven straight days with her. I really got to know her, and it was quite a thrill for me. By the time she left on the plane, I felt that I could tell her stories almost as well as she could.

I loved having the opportunity to work with the opening of Canada, and I hope I can play a role in future foreign development. If Mary Kay needs me, I'll be the first to board the plane. I guess I've got a pioneering spirit.

NANCY TIETJEN lives in Edina, Minnesota, a suburb of Minneapolis. Nancy joined us in October, 1971, and became a Director just fourteen months later. She won her pink Cadillac in eight months! She became a National Sales Director in only two and a half years, another company record! Nancy's 1980 earnings were $187,121.

I was married as soon as I graduated from high school, and following our divorce some years later, I became the sole support of my two daughters, Susie and Christie. With no college education and no secretarial skills, the best-paying job I could find was packing shotgun shells on an assembly line. I worked the graveyard shift, from nine-thirty each night until seven the next morning.

One day, my sister, Jane, called and invited me to a Mary Kay Beauty Show. Instead of saying that she was having a professional Beauty Consultant in to teach a class on skin care, she said, "Nancy, I'm having a makeup party." I told her I wasn't interested. But then she added that she was serving lunch—and she knew I couldn't resist a free lunch.

When I got there, I couldn't believe how beautiful the pink packages and the little mirrors and palettes were. Everything sparkled! Anita Clark (who is now a National Sales Director) was the Consultant, and she was very professional in her presentation. Everybody there bought the complete set, including me—with a postdated check. After the show, Anita said to me, "Nancy, you would be great at teaching skin care for Mary Kay," I was surprised she chose me, and I know I wouldn't be with the company today if she hadn't come over the very next morning.

When Anita told me about the marketing plan, I couldn't believe it! I loved the product, and I loved the fact that the company was founded on the golden rule. When she had explained everything to me, Anita said, "I'm going to be Minnesota's first Director," and I looked at her and asked "Do you think I could be the second?" As it turned out, we were Minnesota's first and second directors.

But that morning, I almost didn't get started. I called my brother-in-law to tell him I was a new Beauty Consultant, and he said, "You're what? You can't do that. You just moved up here, you don't know anyone, you don't even have a car. You'll never make it!" Well, immediately I called Anita and told her I had changed my mind.

She said, "Are you going to let other people make up your mind for you? If you don't try it, how will you ever know?" She promised to train me to do a great Show, and finally I said, "O.K., I'll try it."

I bought a 1963 Mercury for $250 from an ad I saw in the newspaper, and I quit my job at the factory. I gave five Shows a week, each one taking two hours, and right away I was earning more than I had been making working fifty-four hours a week on the assembly line. Of course, when I won my pink Cadillac I no longer had to drive a beat-up old car. I always say those little pink jars mean pink cars. I've had eight Cadillacs so far, and now, as a National, I'll get a new one every other year for the rest of my life.

I love to travel, and not long ago I returned from a trip to the Orient. I'd had gorgeous things shipped over, jade and pink quartz figurines and antiques. My brother-in-law was admiring everything in my beautiful new house—which is equipped with a tennis court and swimming pool—and he said, "Let's make a toast to Nancy." And then you know what he said? "I knew she'd be great!"

RUELL CONE was born and raised in rural Arkansas, the daughter of black sharecroppers who sacrificed to produce a better life for their daughter. Ruell joined the company in April, 1971, as a former teacher with a degree in music education. She became a National Director in August, 1976. Her 1980 earnings were $88,433!

My husband and I had just moved from Little Rock to Atlanta, where he was working on his Ph.D. in theology. We'd put all our savings into a house in a decent area where the kids could go to a good school. When I say we moved, all we had to move was a refrigerator, a used Volkswagen, and my piano. We were just about starving—we didn't have anything. All five of us slept on a trundle bed, and there was no other furniture and no curtains on the windows. We were really poor.

We had decided that I would take care of the kids and do everything so he could be free to study. I had about fifteen piano students, and I also directed the church choir for extra money. I wanted things for my children that I never had. I didn't want them to ever go through what I had gone through as a child. I chopped cotton for ten hours a day out in the hot sun when I was eleven years old—for thirty cents an hour. I always had to work from that time on, and I wanted a better life for my family. I knew there were many things they would never have on a minister's salary, and I didn't want them to have to work as hard as I did to get through college.

The president of the Interdenominational Theological Seminaries was a college friend of my husband, and one day his wife invited me to a brunch. I was so tired of eating the same old things that I said, "Oh, boy, I'm going to have a good meal today." When I arrived at her house, there were all these little pink things on the table. I thought, "Oh, no, one of those make-up parties!" Well, she was the boss's wife, and I couldn't insult her by walking out, so I thought I'd better stay—although I didn't even wear makeup at the time.

But do you know, when that Show was finished I was the first one to say, "I want it all!" I bought the complete collec-

tion, even while I was thinking, "How in the world am I going to pay for this?"

Then, without even stopping to consider, I asked her, "How much do you make selling this?" She told me, and the next thing you knew I had signed a Consultant's Agreement.

When I got home, I thought, "Whatever made me think I could do this? I've never sold anything in my life. How can I tell people what to do?" I called the Beauty Consultant and told her I had changed my mind, and she said, "How do you know you can't do it if you don't try?" I thought that made sense, so I told her I would think about it.

The more I thought about it, the more it looked like an easy way to make money. I had noticed an ad in the Atlanta papers offering $1,000 worth of furniture for only $50 a month, and I wanted to buy that. I thought I could surely sell $50 a month worth of these products. I was convinced that black women needed a skin care program as much as anybody else, and that if they saw the product and tried it, they would buy it. But most of all, I liked the career opportunity the company offered black women. Here was a company founded by a woman who had no color. Mary Kay has only love. I knew that black people would have no problem in this organization. We wouldn't be the "last to be hired and the first to be fired."

My second August with the company, I was already a Director, and at Seminar that year I won my first pink Cadillac! It was a dream come true. I also received a bracelet with thirty diamonds. I'll never forget that—it was a symbol of success. But what I didn't expect was the floor-length Blackglama mink coat they surprised me with because my unit had achieved half a million dollars in sales. When Richard Rogers, the president, brought that coat over and tried to put it on me, I couldn't believe it was mine. I kept asking, "Are you sure this is my coat?" He kept telling me to be still so he could get it on me. But I just couldn't believe it!

I came into this company for money—so I could make $50

a month and buy some furniture. But money isn't what motivates me any more. I am caught up in the whole Mary Kay philosophy, the whole Mary Kay spirit. My dream now is for each one of my Directors to become better than I ever was. I now have two Future National Sales Directors, and I'm so proud of them!

HELEN McVOY, a Dallas resident, joined the company in July, 1965. Seven months later, she became a Director, and in less than a year led her unit to number nine in the nation. One year later, Helen McVoy's unit was number one in all of Mary Kay. In January, 1971, along with Dalene White, Helen became one of our first two National Sales Directors. Her highest monthly commission check was $40,327.63—a company record! Her 1980 earnings were $242,054!

I must confess that before I joined Mary Kay I had always been pampered. My life revolved around golf, bridge, and dinner parties. My husband, Alex, had been a vice-president at Texas Industries, and only when we went broke investing in a manganese mining venture (the Last Chance Mining Corporation—don't you think the name should have given us a clue?) did I even think about watching money. It was a mighty serious financial setback for us, and we really had to watch what we did. But we kept up appearances. We continued to play golf, but we bought a pull cart. We told our friends we were walking for our health, but the truth was that we couldn't afford a ride cart.

About that time, my friend Sally Bryan from California was visiting Dallas, and I met her for lunch. She looked ten times better than she had the last time I had seen her, and I thought she must have had her face lifted. But there were no scars. She told me Mary Kay cosmetics were her secret, and I had to admit I had never heard of the company, although it was right here in Dallas. But I said, "Whatever it is, it's fantas-

tic, and I want some of it." I was ready to order sets for my mother and sisters, too.

But Sally said, "Well, it's not quite that easy, Helen. There's an educational process involved. You can't just buy it—you must have a facial." I couldn't get over her telling me that.

Well, I told my old, dried-up golf friends about it, and we had a Show. And it was such fun! I was also impressed with how much money she had to be making. So I said, "Sally, I'd like to do this, too."

"Helen," she said, "you wouldn't work! How would you find time to play bridge and golf?" But finally I convinced her I was serious, and her Director came over and I signed the agreement.

When I signed, my ambition was actually just to work one week. We were living so frugally, with one child in college and another in a private school, that I could never afford to just impulsively buy a $1.98 pot of ivy for the house. So I thought, "I'll just work one week and buy all the ivy I want, and then I'll quit." On the application, there was a question about how many hours a week I was willing to devote to my career. I figured one Show ought to give me enough money, so I put down two hours.

I wasn't big on working, because I'd enjoyed my life. But my first Shows were so much fun, and it was exciting to come home and pour out all the money on the breakfast room table and count it with Alex. So when I ran out of merchandise I thought, "Well, just one more order—then I'll quit." I went down to the warehouse to pick it up, and that's when I met Mary Kay.

When I saw her there, I walked up and said, "You're Mary Kay and I'm Helen McVoy. I'm going to be a Director." Why I said that, I don't know—it was the furthest thing from my mind.

Mary Kay talked to me for over half an hour that day,

and I could tell she approved of me. She made me feel like a queen! Finally she said, "I think you would be just marvelous. You're just the kind of person we're looking for." Mary Kay said the most wonderful things I'd ever heard in my life, and I believed every word of them. I went right home and began to study my manual from A to Z so I could become a Director.

I went away from that meeting "wound up," and I guess I've been "wound up" ever since. I just love my work—it's not like work at all. Yet today, I suppose I'm one of the highest-paid women in America. And it all started because I wanted a pot of ivy . . .

SHIRLEY HUTTON was probably the best-known television talk show hostess in Minneapolis when she joined the company in October, 1973. In August, 1974, Shirley had skyrocketed to become the Consultant Queen of Recruiting—*and* number four in the Consultant Court of Sales. Shirley has made at least one Queen's Court every year since, and at both the 1979 and 1980 Seminars she was crowned Top Unit Director. In 1979, Shirley became the very first Director to head a unit with sales of more than $1 million—her unit hit $1.3 million! In May, 1980, less than seven years after she joined the company, Shirley became a National Sales Director. Her earnings in 1980 were $211,784.

•

As a local television personality, I was often given complimentary cosmetics. I had them all—the Dina Merrill line, the Zsa Zsa Gabor line, the Polly Bergen line, the Charlie line. Then Marilyn Welle, a Mary Kay Consultant (who is now a National), decided to call me and offer me a complimentary facial. To discourage her, I said she could come to my home at eight in the morning—and she did!

Well, immediately after my facial, I knew that Mary Kay products were much better than anything else I had tried. When I gave speeches to ladies' groups about what it was like to interview celebrities like Omar Sharif and Harmon Kille-

brew (the Twins' superstar), I found myself endorsing the products and giving people Marilyn's name. I even invited five Consultants to be guests on my TV show to demonstrate skin care. I was really indirectly endorsing the product then, too, because it was obvious how much I loved it. Almost eight months went by before Marilyn finally approached me about becoming a Consultant, and one hour later I signed the agreement.

For two and a half years, I kept my job as a television hostess and worked part time as a Consultant, doing two or three Shows a week. After ten months, I was a Director, and I was making as much with Mary Kay as I made in television. Finally, I decided to quit the station and do this full time. My first year with Mary Kay on a full-time basis I made $50,000. Within six years, my annual earnings rose to almost a quarter of a million dollars!

A lot of people were surprised that I would leave a glamorous job as a television personality to enter direct sales. But I just loved doing Beauty Shows. There's something very special about working face-to-face with five or six people. I liked the immediate response that came from that relationship. At first, it was hard to handle some of the remarks people made, such as, "You're not really going to walk away from one of the most prestigious and desirable jobs in Minneapolis to sell cosmetics, are you?" Well, I, too, had a low image of direct sales in the beginning, but I also saw the tremendous potential in Mary Kay Cosmetics. I was thoroughly impressed with the professionalism of the marketing plan, with the people, and with Mary Kay herself. It was a first-class operation in every sense of the term. And it helped when I met businessmen who were also impressed with the Mary Kay organization and what it had done.

I also appreciated the unlimited opportunity. And here was a company telling me how great I was! No television executive had ever said to me, "Hey, great job, Shirley." They didn't want you to think you were doing well, because then *you might ask for a raise. I knew I was doing well, because we were winning with the Nielsen ratings, but I was never praised—and it's a basic human need to be praised. I tell my people, "I think you're just great," and they thrive on it. Everyone loves praise.*

One of the great things about this company is that nobody ever really competes with anyone else. Everyone who reaches a certain plateau can be in the Queen's Court and be a winner. I have only myself to compete with, and this is why we all pull for every Mary Kay person to do well. When somebody really achieves, we don't resent it. Instead, a very healthy attitude is ingrained in each of us in this company: "If she can do it, I can do it, too!"

MARY McDOWELL was sixty-three, widowed twice, and had just recovered from a stroke when she joined the company in February, 1967. She became a Director in July, 1969. Mary was crowned Director Queen of Personal Recruits in 1978 at age seventy-four. Last December, her personal Christmas sales exceeded $17,000—not bad for a seventy-seven-year-old grandmother! At the 1981 Seminar, Mary was crowned Director Queen of Personal Sales.

I've often asked myself why I began to sell Mary Kay Cosmetics. I believe it's because I wanted my own identity. I had been a preacher's wife for several years, and also a professor's wife, and I had never really developed my own identity. My children are highly educated, and I wanted to do something to make them proud of me.

Over the years, I had bought and remodeled nineteen houses and rented them. But my children wanted me to retire from my real estate activities. In fact, they actually thought I was too old to be driving a car! So when I heard about Mary Kay, I decided that I wanted to show my family that I could compete with younger people. I set my goal to become a Direc-

tor—and then I would quit. I didn't need to do it for the money; I just had to prove something to myself.

When I made Director, I received my first letter from Mary Kay, congratulating me and saying, "I'm going to be watching you on the scoreboard from now on." I thought, "Oh, I can't quit now. If Mary Kay is going to be watching me, I've got to climb that scoreboard."

All along, in the back of my mind, I wanted to be a winner so I could prove to my children that I wasn't "over the hill." So every time I was written up in **Applause!** or the newsletters, I'd cut the article out and send it to my children. When I got my first $1,000 check, I made copies and sent them, too.

Wow, I thought I had arrived! I really thought I was on top of the world with my first $2,000 check. And I couldn't believe it when I got my first check for over $4,000. It wasn't the money that thrilled me so—I just wanted to be a winner.

After I had succeeded in the sales end of the business, I made up my mind to be in the Queen's Court of Recruiting. I learned a long time ago how to set goals. I figured out how many I would have to recruit for the year, and broke it down to so many recruits per month, and I started recruiting. I just loved recruiting, because I wanted to give other women the same opportunities I had with Mary Kay. I suppose that's why I was good at it.

I credit this job with having saved my life. I don't know what I would have done without my Mary Kay career. Wherever I go, I talk Mary Kay to everyone. If I see an attractive waitress, I say, "Are you making all the money you think you ought to make? You look like you're worth a lot more money than you're making." The other day, in a dress shop, I noticed a beautiful girl and asked her if she'd ever had a Mary Kay facial. When she said, "Yes, and I love the products," I asked, "Then why aren't you selling them?" Once I even recruited a woman who sat next to me on an airplane. She got so excited *about the opportunity that she wanted to sign up without even having a facial.*

When I was named Director Queen of Personal Recruits in 1978, I was crowned in front of eight thousand people, and they gave me a ten-minute standing ovation. I had the greatest feeling of closeness that night that I've ever experienced in my whole life. I felt like they were all my friends and all loved me. Most of the women were in tears because they were so moved to see somebody my age crowned Queen. Somehow their love reached out to me until I felt like the whole world was full of love. That's why I decided to try for Director Queen of Personal Sales at Seminar 1981 and I MADE IT!

In 1979, 60 Minutes featured Mary Kay, and you can't imagine the excitement it caused when my grandchildren saw me on the program as the Director Queen of Recruiting. One of my grandsons called and said, "Granny, I never dreamed that you'd be the one who would lead the family." And my other grandson told me, "You know, Daddy and Mother always sort of took you for granted. Well, we've come to realize that you really are *somebody."*

Now that you've heard a few of our success stories, I'm sure you can understand why I love my Consultants and Directors. I'm so proud of all the beautiful, capable women who have made my dream come true. Their success is, indeed, "proof of the pudding." As somebody once said, we're "a company that's known for the people we keep." And we think we keep the very best. Mary Kay women are the most loyal and dedicated people in the world. They *define* determination and purpose. They believe that if they work hard enough—if they give enough of themselves—that they will be successful, personally and professionally. And at Mary Kay Cosmetics, they find their lives enriched with friends, accomplishments, and financial security. In 1980, 311 Sales Directors earned more than $30,000; 98 earned more than $50,000!

⌒ 21 ⌒
Spectacular Happenings!

In a recent article about our company, a writer described our Seminar as "a workshop-type convention." Now, *that* has to be the understatement of the century! I told him, "You'd better attend our next Seminar and see what it's all about."

He did. Afterward, he agreed that it was not just "a workshop-type convention." "Mary Kay," he said, "words cannot describe Seminar." But the time has come for me to do what they say can't be done, and put it into words.

Seminar is a multimillion-dollar extravaganza which takes place annually at the Dallas Convention Center. Since past Seminars have sold out almost immediately, we decided to host two back-to-back Seminars (Diamond and Emerald) in January of 1981. We welcomed sixteen thousand women from all over the world to these two spectaculars: To three days of recognition, entertainment, and enlightenment—Mary Kay-style.

For our Consultants and Directors, Seminar is an event eagerly awaited all year long. And we do our best to make sure it's worth the wait! When I've tried to describe Seminar in the past, I've compared it to a combination of the Academy Awards, the Miss America Pageant, and a Broadway opening! Seminar has dazzling awards, competition, drama, and entertainment. Seminar is really a tribute to all the women who make Mary Kay Cosmetics successful—and, I think, unique.

In the midst of the entertainment, we offer approximately one hundred classes conducted by National Sales Directors and the top Sales Directors. These experts address every conceivable subject and their goal is to help each Consultant and Director build a profitable business.

We allow plenty of time for classes, speeches, down-to-business sessions. But without a doubt, the highlight of Seminar is Awards Night! No expense is spared in the elaborate staging, which has all the stardust and glamour of a Cecil B. De Mille production.

Each Seminar has a theme—a phrase that expresses a company philosophy, or a motivational idea. Our January, 1981 Seminar was entitled "Dreams Come True," and what could be more appropriate than a fairy-tale background inspired by the musical, *Camelot*, complete with a castle four stories high, music, and knights and ladies dancing in attendance? Thousands of twinkling white lights made the castle and surrounding greenery sparkle and as the moving score from *Camelot* played, one could not help but think, "Dreams *do* come true!" That's how we want the audience to feel—positively transported to a brighter day and a bigger dream!

At Mary Kay, we have a staff of experts who spend months orchestrating and staging the productions that take place at each Seminar. We present more than thirteen hours of center-stage performances that *overflow* with education, motivation, inspiration, and sheer entertainment. A meticulously prepared script (in 1981, each Seminar script was approximately four hundred pages) is followed behind the scenes as professionally as if Seminar were a $10 million television special! One writer described it as *truly* the "Greatest Show on Earth!" Even the most blasé person can't help but be caught up in the enthusiasm that fills the enormous arena. It's impossible to leave Seminar without taking lifetime memories with you because Seminar offers something to everyone!

The grand opening of each Seminar begins early in the

morning. Long before showtime, though, the arena is filled with early arrivals who want to be sure to get good seats. No matter where you sit in the arena, however, you can still see larger-than-life close-ups of the action on stage, projected on twenty-foot twin screens on each side of the stage. To hold the crowd's interest while the arena fills, professional entertainers lead a sing-along of the most popular Mary Kay songs. The band plays with increasing spirit as the countdown to the official opening ceremony begins. When "Ten Minutes" appears on the giant screens, the crowd cheers and applauds. With growing excitement, the countdown continues: nine minutes, eight minutes, seven.... When I get a glimpse of the crowd from backstage, every single person out there is smiling and clapping in time to the music, until it seems that the whole arena is swaying back and forth.

Seminar 1981 officially opened with music and one of many elaborate multimedia shows. This show featured past Seminars, Queens—a visual memoir that took us all back to the beginning, that storefront seventeen years ago. No one felt the impact of how far we have progressed more than I did as I waited to be introduced. Richard walked onstage to address the audience. I'm sure I don't have to tell you that he received an enthusiastic standing ovation. He welcomed everyone: "Put your troubles away. Forget about whatever might be bothering you and come with us. During the next three exciting days, we will take care of you and your dreams will come true!"

When Richard introduced me, I, too, received a standing ovation. How many times have I spoken to Mary Kay audiences in the past, yet I still get a thrill when that moment at Seminar comes. As I stand there, I'm overwhelmed by the warmth flowing through the arena and I know my love for all of them is returned. Inevitably, everything blurs for a few seconds as my eyes fill with tears and flash bulbs light the arena. I gave a brief welcome before leading the invocation. I call this, "Getting the day started right." Then I dedicated the

Seminar to our National Sales Directors and we were on our way!

At this point, we always begin one of the most exciting visual happenings—the grand march. The DIQs, the Team Leaders, and the Future Directors march from backstage in time to the music, all dressed in their red jackets. For many of these new Mary Kay leaders, this is a first; they have never been in front of such an enormous crowd. In between the marches, several National Sales Directors give their personal stories, each lasting about six minutes. Their unfailing poise is always a source of great joy to me. I am so proud of each and every one of them!

Each speaker tells how she began her Mary Kay career. So many women can identify with our Nationals because they have had the very same thoughts and feelings themselves. One National might say, "I almost didn't come into the business at all because I was terrified of selling! In fact, I used to get headaches when I had to get up and address three people." Each woman in the audience has to think, "And look where she is now!" More than one story has begun, "When I first entered this business, I just wanted to make enough money to pay off a few bills—then I planned to quit. But I got caught up in that Mary Kay spirit, and here I am!"

The stories emphasize one very important message: *"You can be here, too."* Every woman in the audience is told, "There was a time when *I* sat in the back row of this very arena, just like you, and I listened to someone else speak just like I'm speaking now. I said to myself, 'If she can do it, so can I.' And I did it. Remember, it's not where you start, it's where you finish." Every woman there can identify with at least one story, and say to herself, "Yes, and I can do it, too!"

I don't think I've ever heard a speech at Seminar in which the speaker didn't thank somebody for helping her along the way. The Nationals particularly praise the people in their areas. "I wouldn't be here today if *you* hadn't done such a marvelous job. I can't begin to tell you how proud I am of each of you." They learned that the heart of our business is sharing—and so they share the credit for success, too.

As we begin the presentation of awards, these wonderful Nationals take their rightful places helping me present the prizes. During our first opening session, the winners of pink Buicks and Cadillacs are presented with their keys. Since we award so many cars each year to our sales force, only those who qualified during the third and fourth quarters of the year are given the keys at Seminar. This year, our special-effects people created a breath-taking presentation for display of the new models. Each car seemed to float out onstage on a cloud, as a remote-control slide transported the car through a sea of mist to appear center stage in the spotlight. This touch of show business brought oohs and ahhs from the crowd. I couldn't believe the effect—I had never seen anything like it.

The cars themselves are delivered to the local dealers in the recipients' hometowns—nobody has to worry about driving her new car home. But many of our people do drive to Dallas for Seminar, and the Convention Center sets aside a parking lot exclusively for the pink cars. Let me tell you, hundreds of polished pink cars all in a row are quite a sight! It's impossible not to notice them when you're driving by!

The opening session adjourns at twelve-thirty, and it's time for lunch for eight thousand people. During the six-day period of our two Seminars, we serve more than seventy-five thousand meals. It's difficult to believe that eight thousand people could be served lunch in one hour, but the catering service does it—and that's a sit-down meal, too.

After lunch, people adjourn to the meeting rooms in the Convention Center for their classes. The classes start on the hour and run for forty-five minutes. The Seminar programs are sent out in advance so everyone can plan ahead and choose the classes she particularly wants to attend. Included are such subjects as sales techniques, bookkeeping, leadership, goal setting, customer service, recruiting, attitude, motivation, time management, and scores of others. Some are even conducted in Spanish for the benefit of our Spanish-speaking Consultants. The classes are conducted by top Directors and National Sales Directors, and they provide a marvelous opportunity for women to share the ideas and techniques of their peers from all over the world. Our Consultants and Directors take their classes very seriously, making notes and taping the discussions. While everyone enjoys Seminar, it's definitely not a vacation. They come here to learn, and believe me, there's a lot of learning going on while they're in Dallas.

We urge our Consultants and Directors to include their husbands, so special Seminar activities are provided for them. Separate two-and-a-half-hour classes are conducted for the husbands of Consultants and of Directors. Who could be better qualified to conduct these classes than other husbands? I make a brief appearance at each class, and Richard traditionally speaks. The husbands' classes concentrate on ways the men can be supportive of their wives' Mary Kay careers. Every career woman needs the support of her husband, and we've found that the men who attend Seminar become more understanding and more helpful.

We want the husbands to enjoy their trip to Dallas, so we always plan some very special activity. This year we planned a bowling tournament, and brought the winning teams and individuals onstage for awards the final day of Seminar. From their reactions, I think they enjoyed the recognition as much as the tournament!

Seminars also feature big-name entertainers and speakers. Throughout the years, we've welcomed Dr. Norman Vincent Peale, Dr. Robert Schuller and Roger Staubach. For feature entertainment, we've brought in performers such as Tennessee Ernie Ford, Jack Jones, Ben Vereen, Mel Torme, and B. J. Thomas. In the past, we have placed more emphasis on professional motivational speakers than we do now. We've decided that our own people are such great motivators that we really don't need to import motivational speakers. In addition, our people have a message that is exactly right for our audience—

after all, *they've been there!* Our own star Directors and Nationals give Mary Kay people something they can take home and use—and in my opinion, that's the real test of a speaker.

I'm amused at the women who bring their prize mink coats to Dallas and insist on wearing them, even when we have an unseasonably warm January. Of course, any woman who has ever won diamonds wears them. And you can't go anywhere without seeing flocks of red jackets. All of these things—pink cars, diamonds, minks, and red jackets—identify them as Mary Kay Consultants and Directors, but I think that their outgoing, positive attitudes are what make them most memorable.

I take great pride in the comments I hear about our people during and after Seminar. Taxi drivers, waiters, waitresses, bellmen, and all kinds of people will remark how courteous and friendly our people are. We charter buses to provide free transportation to and from the Convention Center, and one bus driver said, "I don't believe it! Every single woman who got off my bus thanked me for the ride!" This may sound like a little thing, but it is indicative of our philosophy. We *are* founded on the golden rule, and I believe we attract a special kind of person because of it. Recently a hotel manager wrote to me:

> . . . *We have hundreds of conventions here, but your people are the nicest and most mannerly I have ever seen in all my years in the hotel business. I have never written a letter like this before, but I just had to tell you. It is our pleasure to welcome back Mary Kay people . . .*

Needless to say, that letter made my day! But, I might also add, it's not unusual.

The only complaint anyone's ever made is that Mary Kay people don't run up big bar bills. In fact, the vast majority of our women will not have a single drink during their visit to Dallas. We never serve alcoholic beverages at any Mary Kay function. Every member of our staff and sales force knows that our rules are not an attempt to regulate their personal lives, but to protect our women. I've known of many unfortunate, and even tragic, incidents that have occurred as a result of drinking. I believe our "no drinking" policy at Mary Kay functions contributes to our professional image and our reputation for being polite. No wonder the city extends a standing invitation to our people. I think the husbands of our Consultants and Directors appreciate our policies, too. They know we're concerned about their wives and that we're committed to taking good care of them.

Seminar must be meaningful to our people because so many come back year after year. For several years now, we've had far more registrations for Seminar than we can accept. Even with room for sixteen thousand people at our back-to-back Diamond and Emerald Seminars, we had to return more than five thousand registrations. Needless to say, people are disappointed when they are turned down, and I receive the saddest letters you have ever seen. Last year, one girl wrote:

> *This was going to be our honeymoon. My fiance and I only have a few days of vacation each, and we arranged to take them at the same time and go to Seminar for our honeymoon. My registration was accepted, but his was rejected! Mary Kay, what kind of honeymoon do you think this is going to be?*

(Of course, we arranged for him to take someone's last-minute cancellation and he was able to attend!)

Without question, the crowning glory of Seminar is Awards Night, which takes place in the arena the last evening. Awards Night is a five-hour spectacular, and let me tell you, spectacular is the only word! Everybody dresses up, with the women in their loveliest gowns, many of them floor length, and our male company executives in tuxedos. We have brief speeches and entertainment, but the excitement really climaxes when we present awards to the top performers for the year.

On this special night, the Director and Consultant Queens

of each category are crowned and honored for their remarkable sales or recruiting accomplishments. They receive diamonds and minks and they're surrounded by a court of women who have also achieved remarkably in that category.

Becoming a Queen in any category is a pinnacle of success for Mary Kay Consultants and Directors. On Awards Night, the members of each court are presented until only the final three winners remain. "Now may we present the Queen and her two runners-up," the emcee announces. "Which of these lovely ladies will be crowned Queen?" Needless to say, pandemonium breaks loose in the arena. Then the second runner-up is announced, and then suddenly, the first runner-up and Queen! As the music crescendos triumphantly, the audience rises to honor the newly crowned Queen. The Queen is presented with a beautiful satin sash, her tiara is placed on her head, her mink coat is draped over her shoulders, a bouquet of long-stemmed pink roses is placed in her arms, and a Queen's diamond ring adorns her finger!

The Queen is seated on her throne and surrounded by her court. The Queen's family is called onstage, too, and her husband is presented with his own diamond ring. Both Richard and I make our congratulatory speeches, and the Queen is asked to say a few words. After she does, the audience rises to give her a well-deserved ovation.

Because every woman in the room understands the challenge of recruiting and sales, they realize how hard the Queen must have worked to reach this moment. The thrill of recognition and praise can be compared to other fields of endeavor. A football player contends for the Super Bowl. An actor vies for an Oscar. The hometown girl dreams of becoming Miss America. And a Mary Kay career woman dreams of becoming Queen. This is her moment of triumph and accomplishment.

The ultimate honor is becoming the Director Queen of Unit Sales. In 1981, the prizes included: two fabulous diamond rings; a gold-and-diamond necklace; a natural ranch mink jacket; a brown shadow mink stroller with Labrador fox collar and cuffs; an all-expense-paid dream holiday in Spain for the Queen and her husband; a diamond bar pin signifying her unit accomplishment; and, of course, her cherished gold bumblebee pin, set with nineteen diamonds. The 1981 Diamond and Emerald Unit Queens further distinguished themselves by becoming members of the elite Million Dollar Club. Because their unit production totaled more than $1,000,000, they were awarded a $5,000 shopping spree at the world-famous Neiman-Marcus in Dallas.

Awards Night comes to a close just before midnight, and a tired but happy crowd leaves the arena to board the buses for their hotels.

The closing day begins in the arena the following morning. Again, a song-and-dance troupe performs. The first major events of the closing ceremony are the Leadership Marches of the top achievers: the Sales Directors, Senior Directors, Future National Directors, and National Sales Directors. Richard always gives a "state of the union" address, in which he deals with such subjects as the national economy, the free enterprise system, and the company's growth.

A highlight of the final morning is the presentation of the Annual Sue Z. Vickers Memorial Award, named to honor our beloved National Sales Director whose untimely death was such a tragic loss to all of us. This honor is presented to Miss Go-Give—the individual who has been the most giving and who has best exemplified the Mary Kay spirit during the past year. The presentation is followed by speeches from Directors of top units and company sales administration executives. And then we close with our traditional candlelight ceremony. It is a very emotional ceremony, and few people in the arena are left dry-eyed. But all good things must come to an end, and we say farewell to another Seminar—until next year.

Since we celebrated our first year in business in our warehouse, we've come a long, long way. Now, many of our Directors' units outproduce our entire first year's sales volume. And

Seminar has become so grand and spectacular I am always a little sad to see it end.

All year long, Consultants and Directors receive encouragement, recognition at weekly sales meetings and in monthly newsletters. We offer sales and recruiting promotions for different levels of achievement—there's always something for which to strive. A reason to set a goal. But Seminar—our spectacular happening—is the most dazzling recognition event we can create. Seminar celebrates the year's accomplishments and lights the way to the future. And as long as women leave Seminar feeling, "I can do it, too—next year I'll be up there," there will always be another year.

⌒22⌒
Leaving a Legacy

Although Mary Kay Cosmetics, Inc., was created as the dream of an individual, it has long since achieved an independent existence. The existence of the company no longer depends on any single individual because it is grounded in a system of values and principles that transcends individuals.

Business analysts often say to me, "Mary Kay Cosmetics to this point has been a business phenomenon. Certainly everything has gone well for this company. *But what's going to happen when you're no longer here?*"

I explain to them that perhaps there once *was* a time when the company depended upon me for its existence. The success of just about any new business hinges on one or two individuals being there every single day. We've come a long way, however, since 1963. Our sales force has tens of thousands of skilled, experienced people, and they are supported by a strong management team. We stopped being a one- or two-person company years ago. We couldn't have grown to our present size if we had not.

You know, Mary Kay Cosmetics isn't the only company that's been identified with its founder. The founders of many American businesses have had very high profiles. Henry Ford is a good example. As large as Ford Motor Company had grown, there were still people who believed it couldn't survive without him—but it did. Another example is Du Pont Chemical. The Du Pont family headed the company for about 150 years. I understand there was concern when an "outsider" became chief executive officer. But today, Du Pont is the largest chemical company in the world. Well-managed businesses *do* survive. If a business can't go forward and prosper without its founder, then I'd say the founder failed to do his or her job in developing a good management team.

I believe our greatest strength at Mary Kay is our people. As I said earlier, we're not only in the cosmetics business— we're in the people business. And, as a people-oriented company, our goal is to offer women opportunity. And these women, in turn, fulfill the needs of other women by teaching them good skin care. In other words, our whole reason for existence is to give people the opportunity to enrich their lives. We follow that principle inside the company, too, and encourage every employee to grow to reach his or her full potential.

Without all those wonderful people, there would be no Mary Kay Cosmetics. But it's important to realize that every company has a natural turnover of people as time goes by. Since that's true, I think it may be that what keeps a company going strong is its philosophy. A company with a good basic philosophy can survive anything—even a major change in its products, as many companies have. Du Pont, for instance, was one of the country's major suppliers of gunpowder from the War of 1812 until World War I. Rockwell International, the large aerospace company, at one time manufactured parking meters and taxi meters. And American Express started out as the pony express! All those companies are doing different things today—but still going strong.

So, as you can see, a company's people will change, and its products may also change over time. What's important is that its *philosophy* remain intact. Every company has a philosophy, and over the course of time, it's this quality that determines the greatness of an organization.

At Mary Kay, our philosophy rests on three beautiful ideas. The first, and most important, is the golden rule. We teach our people to treat other people as they would like to be treated. Sometimes we call this our Go-Give spirit, and we give special recognition to those who show that spirit in outstanding ways. It's a spirit of sharing and caring for the other person. Many outsiders believe it just can't work, but we *know* it works. Our people give cheerfully of their time and experience without thought of what they might receive in return.

The second cornerstone of our philosophy is our belief in the right priorities: God first, family second, career third. I know many corporate heads think we have that list upside down. But we feel that a person can't do a good job if his or her personal life isn't right. We're perfectly satisfied to be in third place.

Our third cornerstone is our belief in the beautiful potential inside every human being. We believe that everyone can be successful, with enough encouragement and praise. So many women have come to us with no confidence at all. "Well, I'll try," they say. "I might—if I can." We teach them to throw those thoughts away and replace them with, "I can, I will, I must!" Over the years, we've found that kind of positive encouragement, together with praise, works wonders. Everyone *can* be great! The seeds of greatness are planted within every human being, and God expects us to reach down within ourselves and bring them into fruition. The countless success stories within our company are proof.

These three beliefs are the basic philosophy of this company, and I feel the future of the company depends not on me, but on these *beliefs!* For that reason, I've made certain that our people *know* how we feel about these things. Everything we do is based on these beliefs. Every new Consultant is recruited on the basis of these ideas and trained to be guided by them. When a Consultant climbs the ladder of success and comes to Dallas for DIQ week, these are the ideas I share with her and her class.

We have had thousands of women who have gone through Director Training. In a sense, each one is the safekeeper of the Mary Kay spirit and philosophy. She is the one I'm counting on to uphold our standards. She must reflect our commitment to honesty and integrity.

It took God a long time to get me ready for the job He had for me. All my years of experience, hard work, disappointment, and trial and error were necessary before I could be guided to form this company. Now that my dream has come true, I am often asked if I will ever retire. Of course, like anyone, I would step down if my health began to fail. Other than that, I will stay as long as I feel our people can be proud of me. Let's face it, there is no fountain of youth—and since we're in the cosmetics business, it's important for me to present a good image. When the time comes that I can no longer do that, I'd be a liability to the company instead of an asset. And this company means too much to me to ever let that happen.

My mother was eighty-seven when she died, and her skin looked wonderful. She didn't start using our skin care products until she was seventy. Since I started using the products at an earlier age, perhaps God will be as good to me. I hope so—I love my work. We're also so fortunate to have as president my son, Richard, who has filled in for me on many occasions and won the hearts of our people. He, one day, will not only fill his job as chief executive officer but mine as well, as motivator of our people.

Whatever the reason, someday I will no longer be here. When that day comes, I know our National Sales Directors will carry on magnificently in my place. Every one of them began as a Beauty Consultant and climbed the ladder right to the top. Our Consultants and Directors know that, so the Nationals serve as wonderful role models for them. I used to refer to these women as "the Mary Kays of the future"—but today, *they already are me*. They carry the torch of our philosophy and standards, so I know that whatever happens in the future, my philosophy will be perpetuated.

Years ago, I worried about what might happen to the company if I was no longer here. I felt a deep responsibility to the thousands and thousands of people involved with Mary Kay Cosmetics. The company had come so far so quickly that I wanted to be sure it could grow and prosper without me. It had helped so many beautiful women that I wanted to know those golden opportunities would always be there. I was possessed with the desire to leave a legacy.

I know now that my legacy is assured. The company has my name, but it also has a life of its own. And its life's blood is the philosophy that many thousands of women have made a part of their lives. They *are* that philosophy of sharing and giving—and that will always live on.